PACIFIC ISLAND BATTLEGROUNDS OF WORLD WAR II:

THEN AND NOW

by

EARL HINZ

Edited by

BUD BENDIX

THE BESS PRESS

3565 Harding Ave.
Honolulu, Hawai'i 96816

Published by

The Bess Press, Inc.
3565 Harding Avenue
Honolulu, Hawai'i 96816

Library of Congress Cataloging-in-Publication Data

Hinz, Earl.
    Pacific island battlegrounds of World War II:
then and now / by Earl Hinz. — 1st edition.
        p.   cm.
    Includes index and illustrations.
    ISBN 1-57306-008-9 (hardcover)
    ISBN 1-880188-94-5 (paperback)
    1. World War, 1939-1945—Campaigns—Pacific Ocean.
    2. Oceania—Description and travel.
I. Title.
D767.9.H56 1995   940.542'6-dc20

Design by Angela Wu-Ki

Printed in Hong Kong

ISBN 1-880188-94-5 (paperback)

Cover photos:

*Then: For three years determined Allied invasion forces faced fanati-
cal Japanese defenders on Pacific islands. Each invasion was like this
one on tiny Peleliu in the Palau Archipelago, where assault troops
had to advance under heavy fire from Japanese defenders hidden in underbrush and caves.*

*Now: While it is peaceful today on most of the islands of the Pacific, the
local residents, such as this Gilbertese fisherman on Betio island with
his catch of the day, still live with reminders of the great battles of
World War II in their backyards.*

TABLE OF CONTENTS

LIST OF MAPS

My personal thanks are extended to the staff of *Pacific Magazine*, Bruce Jensen, Publisher, and Bud Bendix, Managing Editor, for permission to build this book on their original "Then and Now" concept. Individual acknowledgment is made to Bruce Jensen, who created *Pacific Magazine* in 1976, bringing the problems and successes of the emerging countries of the Pacific to the public's attention.

My own association with Pacific Magazine started in 1983 when it accepted my first story on an unscheduled sailboat visit to mysterious Johnston Atoll. Since then, I have authored an almost steady stream of bimonthly Pacific stories for the magazine. The relationship has grown serendipitously over the years, culminating in this book.

When I first conceived of the idea of turning my interest in the Pacific and World War II into a book, I knew I would need help in tying it together. Who better to do that than Bud Bendix, with whom I had worked for years and who has the same topical interests at heart? I sincerely thank Bud for all his assistance—then and now.

Personal thanks are also due Technical Sergeant Dan D'Antonio, USAF 15th Air Base Wing, and Ms. Sandy Miller, Barbers Point Naval Air Station, for their able assistance in supporting my need for firsthand information on the restricted-access Wake and Midway Atolls.

I am indebted to Corydon Wagner, Jr., for providing many of the Peleliu photographs. He was a survivor of that terrible battle and is now an integral part of its history.

And special recognition to my wife, Betty, a World War II bride, who eventually accompanied me as first mate on our sailboat *Horizon* to visit most of the places described herein.

Earl Hinz
Honolulu, Hawaii

PHOTO CREDITS

Unless otherwise noted, all of the black-and-white "Then" photos are products of the U.S. Armed Forces in World War II. Most of them are now found in the National Archives or photo-history sections of the respective armed services. Likewise, unless otherwise noted, all of the color "Now" photos are from my own slide files accumulated in recent years.

CARTOGRAPHIC CREDIT

Except for the concluding map "The New Pacific" on page 97, the charts are the work of Angela Wu-Ki. Their content has been compiled from official sources and personal research by the author.

In late 1990, *Pacific Magazine* published a story about an event that occurred in the Pacific Islands during World War II and a present-day description of the place involved. This prompted a letter from a reader saying how much he enjoyed the piece, particularly since it brought back memories of the time he served in the U.S. Army during World War II and he liked hearing what had happened to the former battleground. The reader suggested that the magazine carry more such stories.

This generated the idea of doing a series of articles about Pacific island battlegrounds of World War II, "then and now." It seemed especially appropriate since we were on the eve of the 50th anniversary of the start of the war in the Pacific. As managing editor of the magazine, I engaged one of our regular contributors, Earl Hinz, to do the series.

Hinz was in the Pacific during the war and had much first-hand knowledge of the events that took place. In fact, he had the unusual experience of serving in both the U.S. Marine Corps and the U.S. Navy, although not simultaneously. Also, since the war, Hinz had taken to his first love, the sea, and he began cruising the Pacific with his wife, Betty, as crew in their 41-foot ketch *Horizon*. This provided him with the up-to-date information needed on the places we eventually selected for our series in *Pacific Magazine*.

We decided that it was unimportant to run the installments in the 13-part series in chronological order. So, it began with the battle of Tarawa, even though the war had started earlier with the bombing of Pearl Harbor. The magazine's editors wanted to save Pearl Harbor for the November/December 1991 issue so that event would be commemorated exactly 50

years later. The other battle that was programmed as an anniversary story was Midway, run in the May/June 1992 issue. In this book, however, the episodes are arranged in roughly chronological order to keep everything in perspective.

There are 12 battles described herein, plus one chapter devoted to the important supply and materiel function that was staged out of what was then known as the New Hebrides. These are places we refer to as the "Pacific Islands," then mostly colonies or possessions of the United States, Great Britain, France, Australia, New Zealand and Japan. Today, most of them have become independent nations in their own right. More specifically, they are the islands of Polynesia, Melanesia and Micronesia, the region served by *Pacific Magazine*. That will explain why you won't find some other important Pacific Basin battlegrounds here such as the Philippines, Iwo Jima and Okinawa.

The descriptions of the battles and present-day life in the islands do not contain all the many details that one would find in historical anthologies, nor are they intended to give that level of detail. Rather, it is the author's intention to provide highlights that might stimulate further reading in the many excellent works that have been published about this momentous time in world history.

Bud Bendix
Honolulu
February 1995

by Bud Bendix

When Japan withdrew its membership in the League of Nations in 1933, there were many who believed this to be a prelude to war in the Pacific. Japanese armies already were in China and there was a great deal of activity elsewhere in what Imperial Japan called its Greater East Asia Co-Prosperity Sphere.

Most important to the Japanese was the acquisition of a number of former German island groups in the Pacific following the start of World War I. They became League of Nations mandates to Japan following the war. These included the Caroline, Mariana and Marshall Islands—virtually all of Micronesia, save Guam, an American possession. These islands, spread over millions of square miles of ocean, gave Japan the kind of buffer zone it needed to build its empire with the creation of the co-prosperity sphere. People came to the islands from Japan to live, work and build. For the islanders, it was nothing new to have foreigners on their soil. Previous "masters" included the Spanish and the Germans. Nor would the Japanese be the last. Americans would be the next occupiers once the war was over.

By leaving the League of Nations, Japan didn't have to play by the rules anymore. Thus, fortification of the islands, making them military bases, was started. Its navy dominated the sealanes. And, even though it was peacetime, no one was allowed to peek behind the empire's curtain in the Pacific to see what was going on. But there was plenty of guessing and most of the speculation was correct. Japan meant to hold onto its mandates and expand even further with open aggression in southeast Asia and the southwest Pacific. To do this, it would be necessary to "neutralize" the United States, strike quickly at British, Dutch and French possessions so those European powers would be more inclined to acquiesce rather than fight and possibly even to invade Australia to assure a solid southern anchor for its co-prosperity sphere.

The plan was activated when planes from a Japanese naval attack force swept over a sleeping Oahu in the Hawaiian Islands on Dec. 7, 1941, and attacked the U.S. fleet in Pearl Harbor. This blow, in addition to other rapid successes in the Philippines, Dutch East Indies, Malaya, Singapore, Guam and New Guinea, brought the Japanese a quick step closer to accomplishing their overall mission. But they grossly underestimated the potential of the Allies, particularly the United States, to recover and turn the tide. This became painfully evident after the Battle of Midway, only six months after the Pearl Harbor raid.

But, that's getting ahead of the story. What follows begins with the attack on Pearl Harbor in 1941 and ends with the battle of Peleliu in 1944. These battles and those in the chapters in between were the key battles in the Pacific Islands war. Each chapter concludes with an inside glimpse of what those places are like today.

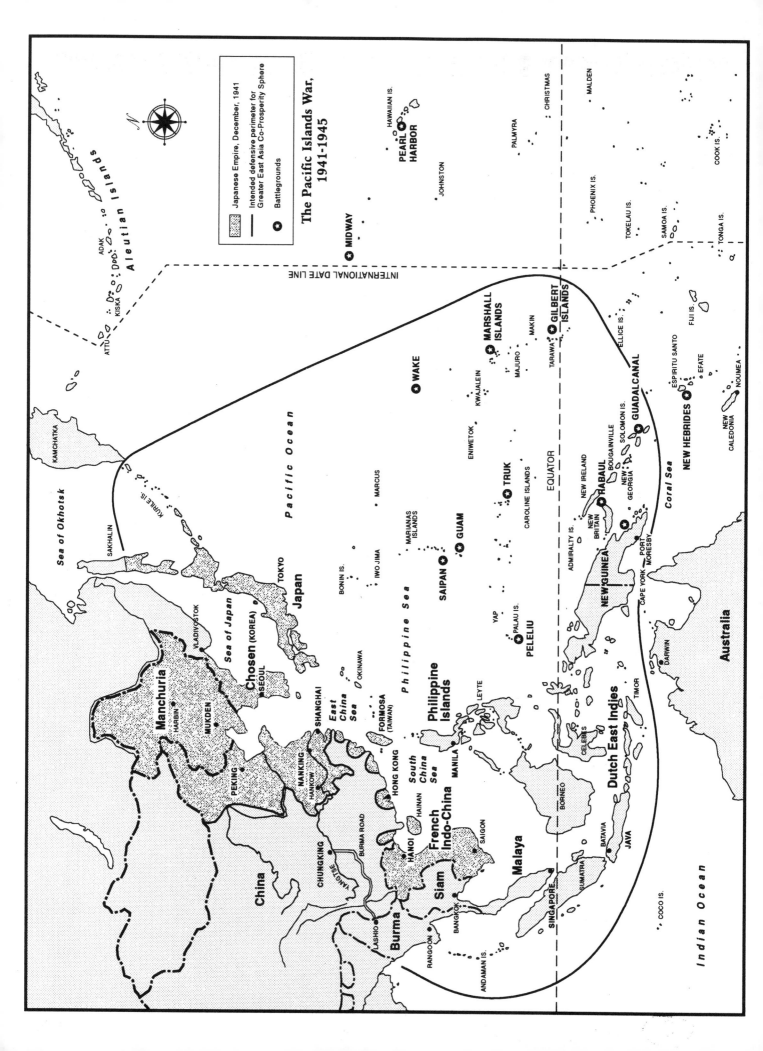

The Pacific Islands War, 1941-1945

Japanese Empire, December, 1941

Intended defensive perimeter for Greater East Asia Co-Prosperity Sphere

✪ Battlegrounds

Aleutian Islands
ADAK
KISKA
ATTU

INTERNATIONAL DATE LINE

✪ MIDWAY

Hawaiian Is.
✪ PEARL HARBOR

CHRISTMAS
MALDEN

PALMYRA

JOHNSTON

COOK IS.

PHOENIX IS.

TOKELAU IS.
SAMOA IS.
TONGA IS.

MARSHALL ISLANDS
MAKIN
✪ GILBERT ISLANDS
TARAWA ✪
ELLICE IS.

✪ WAKE
KWAJALEIN
MAJURO

ESPIRITU SANTO
FIJI IS.
EFATE
NOUMEA
NEW CALEDONIA

Pacific Ocean

ENIWETOK

EQUATOR

✪ GUADALCANAL
SOLOMON IS.
NEW HEBRIDES ✪

KAMCHATKA

Sea of Okhotsk

SAKHALIN

KURILE IS.

✪ TRUK
CAROLINE ISLANDS

ADMIRALTY IS.
NEW IRELAND
BOUGAINVILLE
✪ RABAUL
NEW BRITAIN
NEW GEORGIA

MARCUS

Marianas Islands
✪ GUAM

TOKYO
Japan

BONIN IS.
IWO JIMA

✪ SAIPAN

YAP
PALAU IS.
✪ PELELIU

NEW GUINEA
PORT MORESBY
CAPE YORK

Coral Sea

Vladivostok
Manchuria
HARBIN
MUKDEN

Chosen (KOREA)
SEOUL

Sea of Japan

OKINAWA

Philippine Sea

LEYTE

Australia

DARWIN

PEKING

SHANGHAI
East China Sea
FORMOSA (TAIWAN)

Philippine Islands
MANILA

CELEBES

Dutch East Indies

TIMOR

China
NANKING
HANKOW

HONG KONG
South China Sea
HAINAN

BORNEO

CHUNGKING
YANGTSE

French Indo-China
HANOI
SAIGON

Malaya

JAVA
BATAVIA

Indian Ocean

BURMA ROAD
LASHIO
Burma
RANGOON

Siam
BANGKOK

SINGAPORE
SUMATRA

COCO IS.

ANDAMAN IS.

CHAPTER 1

PEARL HARBOR
The United States Is Plunged into War

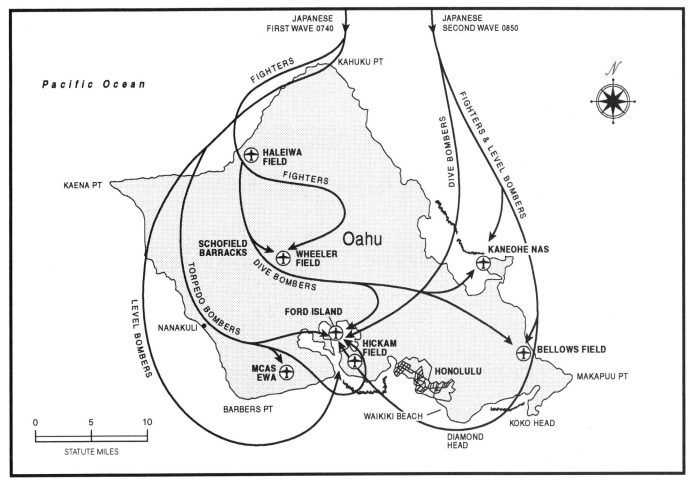

Japanese Operation "Z" - The Attack on Pearl Harbor

AIR RAID, PEARL HARBOR...This is no drill! At 0755, Dec. 7, 1941, 190 Japanese warplanes burst like lightning bolts out of the blue to attack a sleeping Pearl Harbor. They were launched in secrecy from six Japanese Imperial Navy aircraft carriers 275 nautical miles north of Oahu, Territory of Hawaii.

The first wave of "Kate" torpedo and high-level bombers, "Val" dive bombers and "Zeke" fighter aircraft made their ferocious attacks on the ships of "battleship row" in Pearl Harbor. Strafing attacks laid waste to aircraft at the Pearl Harbor and Kaneohe Naval Air Stations, the Ewa Marine Corps Air Base, and the Hickam, Wheeler and Bellows Army Air Corps fields. The first attack lasted 30 minutes and met little resistance. It was devastating.

The second wave of planes came in at 0840 in a finely

tuned choreography of destruction. There were 50 more Kate high-level bombers, 80 Val dive bombers and 40 Zeke fighters. The onslaught continued for another hour, but now met stiffening resistance from surface batteries as well as a few Army Air Corps planes that were able to get in the air from outlying Haleiwa airfield. Then the attacking force retired to rendezvous with the carriers and speed out of harm's way.

Combatant Losses

Japanese losses in this treacherous attack were minimal: 29 airplanes, one fleet submarine, five midget submarines, and a total of 185 persons. (By the end of the war, however, only one of the 30 ships making up the Pearl Harbor strike force was still afloat.) While the Japanese toasted a great strategic

The Arizona *burning after the Japanese attack on Pearl Harbor; 1,103 officers and men lost their lives in this ship. Flaming oil on the water added to the casualties.*

Waikiki Beach, Honolulu, with the Royal Hawaiian Hotel in the background, was fortified with barbed wire to thwart an invasion that never came. The Royal Hawaiian Hotel served as an R & R center for submarine crews during the war.

success against a sleeping target, they failed to realize that they had also sealed the death warrants for 2 million of their own people and Japanese militarism.

American losses were great, as one would expect in a sneak attack—five battleships sunk, three battleships damaged, three destroyers sunk, three cruisers damaged and eight auxiliary vessels sunk or damaged plus 186 aircraft destroyed on the ground.

Personnel losses were heavy—2,428 Navy, Marine and Army personnel and civilians were killed and another 1,223 wounded. On the USS *Arizona* alone, which has become the symbol of the "day that will live in infamy," there were 1,103 officers and men killed or missing.

The city of Honolulu bordering Pearl Harbor, although not a specific target, experienced a significant amount of damage and some casualties. Most of the destruction result-

Sitting ducks on a serene Sunday morning, six battleships neatly moored on the east side of Ford Island feel the initial blows of the first wave of Japanese planes. From left, Nevada, *which managed to get under way but was later beached to save her from sinking;* Arizona, *inboard of supply ship* Vestal *moments before taking her fatal hits;* West Virginia, *which has just taken a torpedo hit (note tracks toward her), and* Tennessee, *inboard of her;* Oklahoma, *which also has been hit, eventually capsized, and* Maryland, *inboard of her, the least damaged of the ships; and oiler* Neosho, *which got away with little damage. At extreme right is* California, *which also tried to get under way but sank. The eighth battleship in Pearl Harbor that day was* Pennsylvania, *in dry dock and hidden by black smoke near center of photo.* Arizona *was a total loss, and* Oklahoma, *although righted, was also declared a total loss. The other six battleships were repaired and saw action later in the war. White smoke at top of photo rises from Hickam Field. This remarkable photo, taken from a Japanese plane, was later captured by U.S. forces.*

ed from friendly fire—improperly fused antiaircraft shells, defective ammunition and inexperienced gun crews. Damage was spotty—a store here, a school there and a number of residences around town.

But the city's fire and police protection services swung into action, aided by civilian volunteers, and Honolulu was put in order for the time being, but it was never to be the same again.

Rolling Up the Shirtsleeves

The American recovery from the attack on the ships and airplanes of Pearl Harbor and the outlying bases was driven by desperation for survival.

Military personnel manned new defenses and patrolled the island for rumored Japanese landings, while others started the difficult task of trying to save hundreds of men trapped in the sunken battleships. The civilian work force took on the challenging task of clearing the drydocks and making temporary repairs on ships to the extent that they could be sailed back to the U. S. mainland for refitting.

Now, with everybody on the alert, Pearl Harbor Shipyard went to work 24 hours a day. It was lit up like a Christmas tree on an island that was otherwise totally blacked out. Everyone knows how the shipyard was able to repair the damaged ships and heal the other wounds inflicted by bombs, torpedoes and bullets in remarkably short periods of time. And it wasn't to be long before the Americans were on the road to Tokyo.

No better example of this rehabilitation work can be found than the USS *West Virginia*, "WeeVee" to her friends. She was hit by at least six torpedoes that slashed her hull like Jack the Ripper. Bombs had collapsed her interior decks into one large cavern. Yet, by May 1942, she was once again afloat and headed into the navy yard. Later she was modernized at a West Coast shipyard and returned to fleet service in 1944. The tenacity of the WeeVee and her crew was amply rewarded when on Aug. 27, 1945, she entered Sagami Bay, Japan, as part of the occupation forces.

Two sailors, left, stare in disbelief as Japanese bombs wreak havoc on the naval air station on Ford Island in Pearl Harbor. The loss of patrol planes hampered the effort at finding the attacking Japanese force.

West Virginia was, in fact, also one of five battleships at Pearl Harbor on Dec. 7, 1941, that took part in the decisive Battle of Surigao Strait in the Philippines in October 1944. The other "returnees" in that battle were *Maryland, Pennsylvania, California* and *Tennessee.*

While the lightning strike of the Japanese attack force put 19 combat vessels out of commission, it proved to be a shortsighted strategic plan. Practically all of Pearl Harbor's repair facilities were left intact—industrial electric power had been untouched, repair shops were virtually undamaged, fire-fighting water was available and the large above-ground petroleum tank farms escaped notice.

The Military Bases Today

World events of the 1990s have reshaped the military in Hawaii as elsewhere. The demise of communism, the inde-

pendence of the countries of Micronesia, the partnership of Japan in Asian defense matters and a more mobile U. S. military have altered Hawaii's role in defense. Pearl Harbor still services all elements of the Pacific fleet as needed, but it is the nuclear submarine force that is the dominant tenant at Pearl.

There no longer is a Naval Air Station at Ford Island. Its airfield is used solely for touch-and-go landings by private aircraft with proper clearances. Hickam has become an Air Force base sharing its major runways with the busy Honolulu International Airport.

The smaller airbases have also undergone changes. The Marine Corps Air Station at Ewa was swallowed up by the large Barbers Point Naval Air Station which, itself, has been scheduled for closing by the Defense Department. Wheeler Field continues as an Army Air Base in support of the Army troops quartered at adjacent Schofield Barracks. The Haleiwa airfield, from which five Army aircraft were able to

A burned Boeing B-17C bomber rests near Hangar Five, Hickam Field, following the attack by Japanese aircraft on adjacent Pearl Harbor.

operate on December 7, no longer exists. Bellows Field on the windward side of Oahu is dormant.

The Kaneohe Naval Air Station was turned over to Marine Corps aviation during the war, but with the closure of Barbers Point it is programmed to once again become a naval air station. Its Marine activities will be transferred back to the West Coast.

The possibility that another attack on Pearl Harbor could occur, probably by long-range missiles, keeps most of the fleet dispersed at sea and in many ports of the world. Nuclear-powered attack and missile-carrying submarines and giant aircraft carriers use Pearl Harbor only for resupply.

Nearby Hickam AFB services world-ranging fleets of B-52 bombers and jumbo C-5 transport aircraft whose mission is in the air and not parked on the tarmac. The rules of war have changed, making dispersal and early warning a necessity for military survival.

Japanese Economic Recovery

When the Pacific war peace treaty was signed on Sept. 2, 1945, aboard the battleship USS *Missouri* in Tokyo Bay, Japan was a thoroughly defeated nation. Its military machine had been destroyed and its economy, once the greatest in all Asia, was in shambles. But it was not to remain that way forever.

A liberal treaty ending the war, a well-disciplined and industrious people, and a "godfather" named Gen. Douglas MacArthur started them on the road to recovery from which they would emerge again, not only as Asia's leading economic force, but an economic force of the entire world.

What Japanese militarists had been unable to accomplish by force of arms has now been accomplished by economic means.

No one knows this better than the people of Hawaii, who have seen Japanese wealth take control of their economy. In its own laid-back style, Hawaii has developed into a tourist mecca for both Western and Asian peoples. Tourism has become its number-one industry, far surpassing the earlier economic accomplishments of agriculture and the military budget. One site that attracts visitors from both sides of the Pacific is the USS *Arizona* memorial in Pearl Harbor. It is one of the few remaining pieces of evidence of the Dec. 7, 1941, attack.

Tourists from Japan

Putting it in perspective, in 1941, Hawaii was visited by 630 Japanese who arrived in 360 single-engine airplanes. They left behind nothing but death and destruction. In 1990, 1.4 million Japanese visitors arrived and left behind $2.5 billion.

On an average day in 1991, 4,000 Japanese visitors arrived in Hawaii on 17 American-made jumbo jets. Japanese visitors on average spend 140 percent more money while in Hawaii than do Western visitors. While they make up only about one-quarter of all visitors to the state, their contributions to the Island economy are significant.

The Japanese also entered the Hawaiian hotel industry in a big way and now own 65 percent of all visitor accommodations there. They have also bought billions of dollars in other real estate. Many say that the investment of Japanese money has been good for Hawaii. But there are probably just as many others who disagree, saying it has added to the already burdensome cost of living and helped create an almost total lack of low-cost housing.

With Success Comes Criticism

Japan's Phoenix-like rise from the ashes has been no less than spectacular, but despite basically harmonious relations with the U.S. and the rest of the world, many feel Japan has failed to shoulder its share of the world's burden as other prosperous nations do. It also has been criticized for the limitations it puts on foreign countries doing business there. Japan has lived so long in isolation, it lacks a sensitivity to the rest of the world's problems.

Although Admiral Matthew C. Perry supposedly opened the waters of Japan to the Western world in 1853, Japan has continued to evade cooperation with that same Western world of which it seeks to be a part.

CHAPTER 2

WAKE ISLAND
Heroic Defense by a Valiant Few

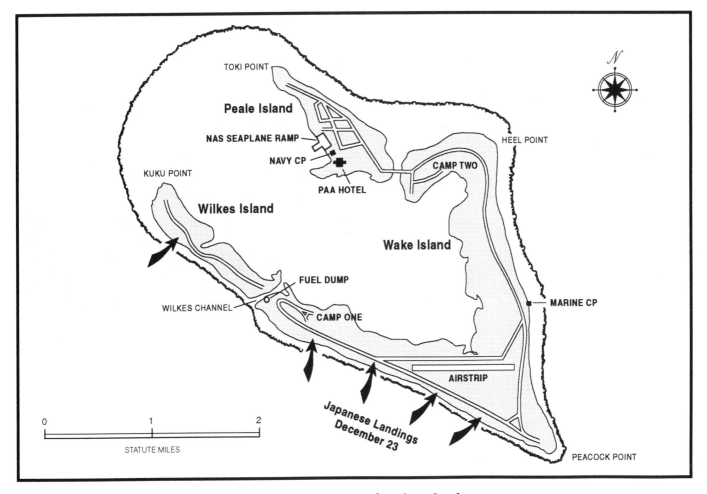

TOKI POINT

Peale Island

NAS SEAPLANE RAMP

NAVY CP

PAA HOTEL

HEEL POINT

CAMP TWO

KUKU POINT

Wilkes Island

Wake Island

FUEL DUMP

WILKES CHANNEL

CAMP ONE

MARINE CP

AIRSTRIP

Japanese Landings December 23

PEACOCK POINT

0   1   2

STATUTE MILES

Japanese Capture of Wake Island

Wake Island, at best, is a desolate, waterless atoll in the western Pacific totally lacking in resources other than hot sun and coral sand. Yet today, this barren mid-Pacific atoll has been made a U.S. national historic landmark in recognition of a most heroic World War II battle.

Wake Island is not its proper name since it is truly an atoll composed of three islands—Wake, Peale and Wilkes—that, collectively, are the tops of an inactive volcano long since subsided and eroded away. The three islands form an east-pointing arrowhead with Wake at the apex and Peale and Wilkes as the barbs. Only the prolific coral polyps have kept Wake's head above water over endless years. Inside the barrier reef and its three islands, the lagoon is a maze of coral heads to hinder its use by man.

Discovered by the Spaniard Alvaro de Mendana in 1568

and annexed by the United States in 1899, Wake did not figure in world affairs until the 20th century.

In 1935, Pan American World Airways System recognized Wake's geographic importance to the coming age of flight and developed it as a base for trans-Pacific commercial seaplane flights. They located their pre-World War II seaplane facilities and land support operations on Peale on the windward (northeastern) side of the atoll.

Shipping facilities were located across the lagoon on Wilkes, on the leeward side of the atoll. It is the only island having reasonable protection from heavy seas. Wake Island, itself, did not figure in Pan American's early plans, although it later became the land-plane runway.

The laborious job of converting this treeless, waterless lump of coral into a modern seaplane facility got underway in

Pan American Airways' Hawaii Clipper *moored off the Peale Island pier in the late 1930s.*

May 1935. Logistics problems were imposing, since everything from cement to construction workers had to be shipped by water from the United States to Wilkes and then transported across the lagoon to Peale. Even so, by November 1935 the first westbound *China Clipper* was serviced at new facilities while its passengers enjoyed an overnight stay in a first-class hotel. The Pacific's air age had begun.

A Strategic Location

Wake's geographic location and the success of Pan American's Clipper service did not go unnoticed by the two major Pacific Rim powers. The United States increasingly looked on Wake as a potential gigantic "aircraft carrier," patrol plane base and defensive position strategically located inside the periphery of Japanese-held islands.

Japan saw it as a highly dangerous threat to their Greater East Asia Co-Prosperity Sphere, which now had secret island bases in surrounding Micronesia. Once development started, Japan maintained regular aerial surveillance of it from the neighboring Marshall Islands. Worried though they were, they could do nothing politically to stop the development.

Although the United States declined to fortify Guam, 1,300 miles farther west, so as not to antagonize the Japanese, they thought differently of Wake and ordered construction of a naval air station there.

A civilian construction team arrived in early 1941, and nearly 1,200 workers began building military installations. A construction camp was set up on Wake near the Peale pass.

Runway construction was started near the center of Wake and a Marine guard camp was built at the far end near the Wilkes channel. A seaplane base for the Navy's Catalina flying boats was built alongside the Pan American facilities at Peale. All work was destined for completion in mid-1942, a schedule that was soon to be altered by the Japanese.

By October 1941, with base construction progressing well, a Marine defense battalion plus some Navy civil engineers and Army Air Corps communications personnel were landed. They proceeded to install military defenses and communications and to stockpile munitions and other combat supplies.

Pleas from the Marine commander, Maj. James Devereux, to get heavy construction help from the civilian contractor were rejected by the Navy command. That meant much backbreaking work had to be done by the Marines themselves, who lacked proper equipment for such construction. Nevertheless, they persevered in the hot sun and were ready to receive their air defense complement of 12 Grumman F4F Wildcat fighter aircraft on Dec. 4, 1941.

Carrier-based Douglas SBD Dauntless dive-bombers attack Japanese-held Wake Island on October 5 and 6, 1943, as part of a continual harass-ment of the island by air and sea to prevent its use by the Japanese as an advance base.

The wreck of the Suva Maru. *She was hit by two torpedoes from an American submarine while attempting to supply the blockaded and starving Japanese on Wake in July 1943. She was run on the reef to prevent sinking. Picture, circa 1954.*

The Japanese Invasion

World War II came without warning to Wake at 1158 on Dec. 8, 1941 (west of the dateline time), with a Japanese bombing offensive directed against it by aircraft from the Marshall Islands.

At that time Wake's total defense was composed of 449 Marines, a smattering of Navy and Army personnel and the 12 fighter airplanes. Ground firepower consisted of 3- and 5-inch gun batteries, .30- and .50-caliber machine guns, grenades and the Marines' faithful old 1903 .30-caliber Springfield rifles. Some vital logistics support was furnished by the 70 Pan American personnel (mostly Guamanians) and the 1,146 construction workers.

The rusting remains of a Japanese light tank are inspected by two civilian residents of the atoll. Picture, circa 1954.

After three days of bombing, an invasion attempt was made on December 11 by the Japanese Fourth Fleet from Truk under Admiral Kajioka, but was rudely beaten off with Japanese losses of two destroyers and an estimated 700 casualties. The invasion fleet retired to the Marshall Islands to lick its wounds. The defenders cheered, but not for long. Wake was not to be left alone.

Bombers from the Marshalls attacked the atoll every day in preparation for another invasion attempt. On December 22, the last two Wildcats were destroyed and aviation unit personnel joined the defense battalion as infantrymen.

The invasion fleet, much stronger this time, returned on December 23. It was reinforced by two aircraft carriers with their screen of cruisers and destroyers that had been part of Pearl Harbor attack force on December 7. The assault landing group itself was made up of more warships, transports and landing craft, which succeeded in putting ashore a predawn landing force of 1,000 Japanese marines despite heavy opposition.

Wake fell at 0730 on December 23 after 15 days of desperate fighting[1]. American dead totaled 122, with 12 airplanes lost. The Japanese lost 820 men, plus 11 naval ships and 21 airplanes.

Initially, life on Wake under the Japanese was not decidedly different than before the war started. The prisoners were well fed from U.S. food supplies and were employed in continuing the construction work and teaching their captors how to operate the heavy construction equipment.

[1] The Pearl Harbor command, in spite of their own problems, did not completely forget the defenders of Wake. They created a relief force under Admiral Frank Fletcher built around the carrier *Saratoga*, which had to come from San Diego. Two other task forces built around the carriers *Lexington* and *Enterprise* would make diversionary attacks on the Marshalls and cover the approach back to Hawaii.

In all this planning, there was real and justified concern about losing even one American carrier. The relief force was organized and able to get within 425 miles of Wake by December 23, but by then it was too late and it was called back to Hawaii. The final roll of the dice had occurred.

A twin-mount Japanese naval gun is nearly lost in the tropical overgrowth of time. Picture, circa 1954.

In mid-January 1942, all the American military forces, along with the prominent civilians, were evacuated by ship. A second group of civilians was evacuated at the end of September, leaving behind 98 civilians. The latter were summarily executed on Oct. 7, 1943, ostensibly for establishing contact with the Americans. A more likely reason was a shortage of food brought on by a tight U.S. sea and air blockade.

By 1943, the Japanese garrison had grown to 4,100 troops, but never became larger because of the blockade. In fact, starvation and American bombings finally reduced the Japanese forces to 1,242 persons by the time of the surrender in 1945.

The Imperial Japanese Navy was not given any opportunity to use Wake in the manner it had intended—as a link in the Tokyo-to-Marshall Islands defensive frontier. During their 3-1/2 years of occupation of Wake, they were repeatedly attacked by American carrier aircraft, land bombers and later by ships' guns. What had been thought by the Japanese to be

an asset had turned into a liability. In the end, no reinvasion by the United States was necessary. The atoll was simply bypassed until the end of the war, when on Sept. 4, 1945, it again became U.S. property.

The Postwar Period

Wake's postwar history isn't nearly as exciting, but it is just as varied. The U.S. Navy occupied the island until 1947. Then the Federal Aviation Administration took it over for 25 years as a refueling stop for land planes, which had replaced flying boats, as PanAm quickly revived its trans-Pacific operations.

Transocean Airlines took over the base-keeping task as well as providing additional trans-Pacific airline service. The U.S. Coast Guard installed a Loran-A radio-navigation station on Peale, and the U. S. Weather Service established a reporting station on Wake that has been in continuous operation ever since.

With the advent of long-range jet airplanes, Wake was no longer needed for refueling and the FAA turned it over to the U.S. Air Force in 1972. Today's operations are handled by the USAF 15th Air Base Wing out of Hickam Air Force Base. Services include host support for tenants, maintaining an airfield facility for contingency operations such as the recent Gulf War, in-flight emergency recoveries, limited refueling and transient base support for government and civilian aircraft, limited maritime capability for cargo vessels and assistance in maritime emergency recoveries.

For a time in 1975, international attention was again focused on Wake as thousands of Vietnamese refugees were housed there, some for as long as four months until space in U.S. refugee centers could become available. Wake's strategic location continues to make it important to national affairs in spite of (or, maybe, because of) its isolation.

CHAPTER 3

MIDWAY
The War's Early Turning Point

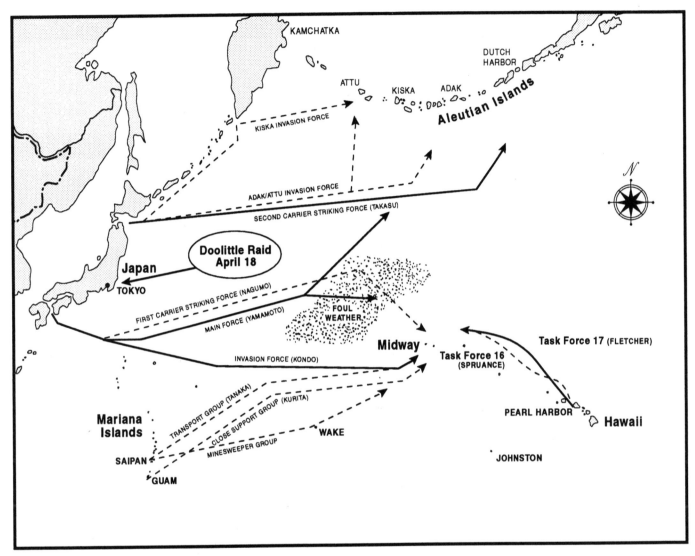

Japanese Operation "MI" - Midway Islands Attack

Riding the crest of multiple sea victories in the Pacific, the Japanese Navy in early 1942 appeared invincible. Pearl Harbor had been devastated. Japanese Admiral Nagumo, with four carriers from his Pearl Harbor attack force, roamed the South Pacific. They freely attacked islands of the New Guinea archipelago and Darwin, Australia. They even proceeded into the Indian Ocean to sink cargo vessels and British warships in Ceylon's (now Sri Lanka) waters.

The Allies, in fact, were badly in need of some good news from the Pacific fighting front. It finally came from a most daring operation. On April 18, Tokyo was struck by American bombers, which President Roosevelt said came from "Shangri La."

When secrecy was lifted, it turned out that they had been launched from the carrier *Hornet*, 700 miles east of the Japanese homeland. The daring raid by 16 B-25 Mitchell bombers, led by Lt. Col. James Doolittle, served its purpose well, boosting American morale even though the physical damage done to Tokyo was minimal.

On the other hand, Japanese morale sagged when they learned that their invincible military could not protect their homeland from attack. Imperial planners set to work to devise a strategy to prevent further attacks on the home islands.

The carrier Hornet *running into heavy seas while steaming at high speed en route to the launch point for its deckload of Army North American B-25 Mitchell bombers destined to bomb targets in Tokyo. President Franklin D. Roosevelt publicly referred to this seagoing base as "Shangri-La."*

The Japanese aerial attack on Eastern Island started at 0630 on June 4 and continued for two hours, in spite of heavy ground fire. Most ground facilities were severely damaged. Although additional land target attacks were planned by the Japanese, U.S. planes attacked their carriers, preventing further damage.

Midway Becomes the Target

Admiral Yamamoto, commander-in-chief of Japan's combined fleets, reviewed the results of their campaigns in 1941 and early 1942 and laid further plans for expanding the navy's destruction of Allied forces on land and sea. The naval general staff on May 5 approved his plan to attack and occu-

py Midway Atoll. Its purpose was to block any additional Doolittle-type raids against the homeland by the United States and to prevent any interference with Japan's planned expansion of its Greater East Asia Co-Prosperity Sphere.

With great enthusiasm, but a noticeable lack of hard intelligence, the plans went forward for the occupation of Midway. But Yamamoto had already forgotten his prophetic

The mortally wounded Yorktown *takes a severe list to port as sailors continue to abandon ship. Destroyer* Balch *stands by to perform personnel rescue.*

Midway Atoll, November 1941. Developed Eastern Island is in the foreground. Sand Island, background, was developed after the war started. Midway was a major submarine support base as well as an aviation center.

statement on the Pearl Harbor attack: "I am afraid we have awakened a sleeping giant." It was no longer sleeping.

Midway has but two sandy islands, Eastern and Sand, with a total land area of 2 square miles surrounded by a reef 5 miles in diameter. Prior to the arrival of Commercial Pacific Cable Company in 1903, the islands were nothing more than sand, coconut palms, shipwrecks and thousands of "gooney birds" (Laysan albatrosses).

The cable company built its installation on a corner of Sand Island and over succeeding years made the island more habitable by planting *Casuarina* (ironwood) trees and other flora. There were no other developments until 1935, when Pan American Airways arrived to build a refueling base for its trans-Pacific Clipper service.

Left: This major hangar on Eastern Island was heavily damaged during the initial raid by Japanese carrier-based planes on June 4, 1942.

Bottom: Sailors check out a heavily damaged Grumman TBF Avenger torpedo bomber on Midway. This was the first action the new Navy plane saw in the war. Of the six present on the atoll during the battle, five were lost. The Avenger compiled an outstanding combat record throughout the rest of the war and was the same type flown by U.S. president-to-be George Bush.

The first garrison of 20 U.S. Marines arrived on Sand Island in 1904 and departed in 1908. A permanent garrison of 850 Marines took up station on Eastern Island in June 1940 and a fully manned naval air station was operating on Eastern by August 1941.

For his Midway attack, Yamamoto assembled three forces—the main body with 18 ships, including the superbattleship *Yamato*; the First Carrier Striking Force, under Admiral Nagumo of Pearl Harbor fame, which included the four veteran Pearl Harbor strike carriers, *Akagi*, *Kaga*, *Soryu* and *Hiryu*; and the core invasion force with 77 combat, troop transport and auxiliary vessels. His carriers bore 325 planes, including 96 of the finest fighter plane of the period, the

Zero. His planes carried torpedoes far superior to any the United States had in its inventory.

In comparison, the United States was able to field only 27 surface ships, including *Enterprise*, *Hornet*, and the severely damaged but temporarily repaired *Yorktown*. As for planes, the Americans had 348, if you include the hodgepodge of planes that were to operate off Eastern Island runways. They ranged from obsolete Brewster Buffalos to unproven planes such as six new Navy TBF Avenger torpedo bombers and four Army B-26s hurriedly equipped with torpedo racks at Pearl Harbor.

Yamamoto's strategy was simple: Overwhelm the Midway forces in a lightning attack and occupy the islands after a brief battle. He had no idea where elements of the U.S. fleet were, but he was prepared to take them on also.

Unbeknownst to him, the U.S. Navy had cracked Japan's operational radio code and was able to follow its evolving Midway attack plan. This allowed Nimitz to position his outnumbered carriers under Adms. Raymond Spruance and Frank Fletcher, and their inferior airplanes where they would be most effective, and hold them in readiness until the appropriate moment.

Then it became a waiting game with the strategists, Yamamoto on *Yamato* and Nimitz at Pearl Harbor. Japan had to make the first move.

The Battle Is Joined

The actual fighting occurred in three approximate phases—

Right: Once the two carrier fleets found each other, their airplanes became totally dedicated to the destruction of the other's vessels. Following bombing and torpedo runs, aircraft engaged in strafing operations on their vessel targets.

Bottom: The Doolittle raiders bravely take off from the USS Hornet *under adverse sea conditions after the fleet had been observed by a Japanese picket vessel. The distance to Tokyo was then greater than planned, making difficult the B-25's recovery plan to Chinese airbases.*

the attack, the counterattack and the rout. On June 3, Navy and Army reconnaissance planes spotted elements of the invasion force and nine B-17s attacked it late in the afternoon followed by four Catalinas in a night torpedo attack. Damage was minimal in both attacks.

At 0430 on the fateful day of June 4, 1942, the Japanese launched their attack planes from the strike force. These were met 30 miles out of Midway at 0615 by ground-based interceptors, which proved ineffective. The attack force bored in on Midway and caused severe damage to facilities and aircraft on Eastern Island. Meanwhile Navy TBFs and torpedo-carrying Army B-26s attacked *Akagi* while American bombers attacked the other carriers. There were no hits. The Japanese had won the attack phase.

The counterattack started at 0706 when *Enterprise* launched its own aircraft followed shortly afterward by planes from *Hornet* and *Yorktown*. Their timing was fortuitous, as they caught Japanese carriers with many planes on their decks being refueled and rearmed.

By 0830, all four Japanese attack carriers were under a furious attack by planes from the three U.S. carriers, as well as the remaining Midway-based aircraft. *Akagi* was put out of action first, by 1043.

In return, *Hiryu* airplanes attacked *Yorktown* at 1200, severely damaging it so it had to be abandoned. A late afternoon attack by planes of *Enterprise* and *Hornet* hit *Kaga* and *Hiryu* again. *Soryu* had sunk at 1915 from earlier attacks. *Kaga* sank at 1925 and *Akagi* was abandoned at 2000 and later sank. *Hiryu* was abandoned at 0230 the

next day and also sank. The Japanese First Carrier Striking Force was no more.

The Rout Begins

The rout of the Japanese forces began before dawn on June 5 when Yamamoto canceled the Midway operation. Midway-based aircraft and planes from *Enterprise* and *Hornet* continued to pound the retreating fleet. Soon, only scattered Japanese ships were found. The biggest target was the cruiser *Mikuma*, which was furiously attacked. It sank at sunset on June 6. But the Japanese were still not through.

At noon on June 6, the Japanese submarine 1-168 found

the wounded *Yorktown* with a salvage crew valiantly attempting to save it with the aid of the destroyer *Hammann* alongside. The submarine fired a series of torpedoes at this double target, one hitting and sinking *Hammann* immediately and others striking *Yorktown*. Without external power for pumps, the carrier had to be abandoned again. She succumbed to flooding and sank during the night.

The battle of Midway was fully over by noon on June 7.

Combat ship losses in this one-sided battle were: Japanese, four carriers and one cruiser; the United States, one carrier and one destroyer. Additionally, the Japanese lost 332 planes and 2,500 personnel, while the Americans lost 147 aircraft and 307 personnel. The Japanese lost the cream of their pilots in the Coral Sea and Midway battles, a result from which they would never recover.

The combat role of Midway began and ended with this one great battle that changed the course of the war in the Pacific. But her role in the war wasn't over. Soon a submarine base and airfield were added at Sand Island to complement the Eastern Island facilities, and the base continued to provide valuable support for the rest of the war.

Midway at Peace

Following V-J Day, Midway personnel were demobilized and the entire command decreased to only 250. A peacetime operation then took over and by August 1946, Navy families were being given quarters on Sand Island along with their men.

In July 1958, Midway assumed a new role as a base for an airborne early warning squadron as the cold war heated up. Those operations lasted until May 1970 when, again, there was a downturn in Midway activities. Dependents were no longer allowed to accompany Navy personnel on new one-year duty assignments.

The atoll was designated a national wildlife refuge in April 1988 and the undersea cable service, which was Midway's beginning, was terminated in September 1990. Only a small detachment of Navy personnel and a supporting base contractor were left to tend the facilities and provide succor to airmen and mariners who stopped at the atoll.

Now, even that thread of Midway's contribution to the security of the United States has changed. The federal government decided that Midway was no longer needed for national defense, and the naval air facility was closed in October 1993. Before the atoll is finally turned over to the Fish and Wildlife Service to continue as a wildlife refuge, it will first have to be cleaned up of dump sites, underground fuel tanks and other relics from a lifetime of military occupation. The atoll has now been returned to its original inhabitants, the gooney birds.

CHAPTER 4

GUADALCANAL
It Hung by a Thread

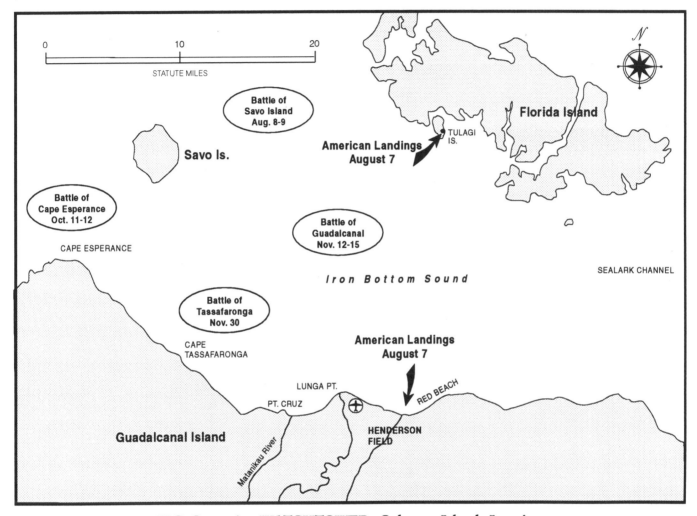

U.S. Operation WATCHTOWER - Solomon Islands Invasion

Probably no battle in World War II's Pacific Theater hung by such a slender thread of success than did the early struggle for Guadalcanal Island in the Solomon Islands.

This was due to long, tenuous supply lines with only skeleton naval forces available for sea transport and combat. It also suffered from a command dispute between Gen. Douglas MacArthur, who claimed he needed the same resources to turn back the Japanese from their New Guinea invasion, and Adm. Ernest King, U.S. chief of naval operations, who saw the Japanese presence on Guadalcanal as a far greater threat to the whole southwest Pacific and one that must be nipped in the bud.

A compromise gave MacArthur responsibility over New Guinea and related areas and Admiral Nimitz responsibility

over the Solomon Islands campaigns.

The early British administration of the Solomon Islands Protectorate had settled itself in 1884 on the island of Tulagi, a place well sheltered from the strong southeast trade winds and one having a good harbor.

At the start of World War II, the invading Japanese easily captured it and made it their headquarters. Then they moved across Sealark Channel (later to be known as Iron Bottom Sound) and started construction of an airstrip on the plains of Guadalcanal. They must have thought the little airstrip would go unnoticed by the Allies, who were busy fighting off the New Guinea invasion. The U.S. Navy, however, didn't take kindly to this little threat and set out to deny its use to the enemy and make it into an air base for its own use.

Battle-scarred Henderson Field in August 1942 shortly after it was captured by U.S. Marines. The airstrip (running diagonally) has been repaired—a daily job—for use. U.S. combat planes can be seen on both sides of the strip at the left. The Lunga River is seen at the top of the photo.

Marine Corps officers and enlisted men take a rare moment of relaxation at the building used as a headquarters at Henderson Field in 1942. Later, the structure had to be replaced after a near-miss from a Japanese bomb rendered it useless. A combat plane can be seen in the distance just over the roof at right center.

Unwittingly, perhaps, the ensuing battle for Guadalcanal actually helped MacArthur's cause in New Guinea because it deflected enormous numbers of Japanese air, ground and naval forces from that campaign, giving MacArthur much-needed relief.

To the Japanese Command it became an almost bottomless pit for their airplanes based in Rabaul. The 1,000-mile roundtrip left little fighting time for the aircraft and fatigued the pilots greatly. Postwar estimates reported 263 Japanese planes lost in the first month of the battle versus 101 American planes lost.

The Japanese eventually built air bases in the northern Solomons, such as at Kieta and Munda, and reduced flight time, but by then they also came under the guns of American aircraft from Guadalcanal.

Five Japanese tanks lie knocked out on a sand spit across the mouth of the Matanikau River after heavy fighting in late 1942. Savo Island is seen on the left horizon.

All for an Airstrip

The sole prize in the long seven-month battle for Guadalcanal was really only the little airstrip. Violent naval battles would be fought, air combat would be a daily affair and American ground troops would encounter fanatic Japanese soldiers, malaria, endless rain and mud in their drive to keep possession of it.

The initial landings of the 1st U.S. Marine Division at Guadalcanal, under the command of Gen. Alexander Vandegrif, took place on Aug. 7, 1942, at Beach Red, a few miles to the east of the landing strip. Here men and materials were unloaded from Navy transports with no enemy opposition. (Beach Red was to be the principal landing for months to come, but rarely was there no opposition later.)

The airstrip, later named Henderson Field, was occupied by the Marines on the second day and held thereafter in spite of furious counterattacks by Japanese reinforcements that had arrived on the ships of the "Tokyo Express." Under fire from Japanese ground troops, ships and planes for months, the field operated on a shoestring for the entire campaign, the enemy never realizing how close it came to recapturing it.

Henderson Field was nothing but weeds, coral, mud and bomb craters throughout most of the battle. It was manned by an assortment of U.S. Marines, sailors, soldiers and Army airmen who flew whatever planes they could get their hands on and keep bolted together.

These aircraft came to be known as the Cactus Air Force, after the code name, "Cactus," given to Guadalcanal. They attacked Japanese ground positions, landing craft, transport ships, aircraft and combat vessels in furious battles for the survival of Henderson Field.

Early Japanese intelligence believed there was only a small contingent of Marines on Guadalcanal, so in their initial counterattacks they sent minimal reinforcements to drive the Marines out. They were wrong. There were 11,000 troops of the 1st Marine Division ashore and well dug in before Japanese counterattacks could begin.

Japanese intelligence also failed to learn of the meager supplies the Marines had ashore because of a dearth of U.S. Navy combat ships and planes to protect supply ships. The combatants were already in an intelligence trap that was to plague both sides for the full seven months of the battle. Both sides were fighting blind and suffering extensive losses because of it.

Night Naval Engagements

While American ground forces battled ever-increasing numbers of Japanese, the naval forces slugged it out in the waters off Guadalcanal.

The first major naval battle in the Guadalcanal campaign was the battle of Savo Island, Aug. 8 and 9, 1942. It was a disaster for the Allies, with the U.S. losing three cruisers and Australia another. HMS Canberra, *above, is afire and mortally wounded, as U.S. destroyers* Blue, *left, and* Patterson *take off 680 survivors from the Australian cruiser. Although* Patterson *survived the campaign,* Blue *was lost in the Battle of the Eastern Solomons two weeks later.*

Japanese naval tactics, particularly in night encounters, were far superior to those of the Allied forces, and this led to the famous Battle of Savo Island, later described as the worst sea defeat in U.S. history. Without the help of radar, a small Japanese cruiser force under Admiral Mikawa made its way in the dark of night into Iron Bottom Sound, where elements of the U.S. and Australia naval forces were on routine patrol off Guadalcanal.

In the melee that ensued, the Japanese were able to fire point blank at targets only three miles away, in the end sinking or disabling most of the Australian and American ships.

But Mikawa chose to retire instead of following his original plan to attack the U.S. transports only a few miles farther into the sound. Had he done so, Japanese ground troops could have, in all probability, driven the Marines off Guadalcanal.

Two months later, surface forces again engaged each other in a night battle off Cape Esperance. The Allied forces were now better prepared and more alert and intercepted the "Tokyo Express" bringing in more men and supplies at midnight. In the ensuing battle the Japanese fleet took a licking that evened the score with the Savo Island engagement, with both sides losing an equal number of ships—24.

In the end it was the U.S. staying power in the naval battles that followed that made the difference. The Allies were able to replace many ships and keep sizeable forces in the battle.

The End in Sight

On December 9, the 1st Marine Division was relieved by the 2nd Marine Division under Gen. Alphonse DeCarre and the 35th Army Division under Gen. Lawton Collins, which together pressed forward both east and west on the island, driving the Japanese to the sea. It was known that Japanese replacements were being landed on the island but not how many. In fact, after a couple of months, American and Japanese forces were about equal in number, but where were they? U.S intelligence could not say. Few Japanese surrendered.

The Japanese command, realizing that it could not stave off defeat, then started secretly evacuating troops at night from the west end of Guadalcanal. By Feb. 8, 1943, no active Japanese troops were left on the island, only the 24,000 dead they left behind. The American death count was 3,000 men.

The battle of Guadalcanal was now over, but the battle for the Solomon Islands continued. To supply the northern Solomons offensive, a massive supply dump had been created at Point Cruz, a few miles west of Henderson Field. This was the only place along the island's windward shoreline where topography was at all favorable for any kind of harbor operations. The indigenous name for Point Cruz was Naho-ni-ara, meaning "facing the trade winds," and from this came the name Honiara for the present capital of the Solomon Islands.

The 'Canal Today

After the Allied Forces left the Solomons, the large supply dump with its network of Quonset huts and hordes of left-over war equipment became an attractive place for the

Right: The carrier Hornet, which helped deliver the first blow against Tokyo in April 1942, is abandoned on Oct. 26, 1942, in a sinking condition, during the Battle of Santa Cruz Islands. Destroyers are assisting with rescue work. Hornet sank the next day after suffering 111 killed and 108 wounded.

Bottom: Japanese warriors were not the only enemy on Guadalcanal. This crocodile chased Pfc Roy Morriss from the river in which he was swimming. His companions shot the reptile.

British colonial administration to rebuild its headquarters rather than on bombed-out Tulagi. They maintained a colonial administration there until 1978, when the Solomon Islanders gained full independence.

It was only natural that the new nation of Solomon Islands would keep Honiara as its capital in spite of the lack of a natural harbor. They reasoned that harbors can be built by man and that is what was done. Point Cruz was reshaped many times by bulldozer and dragline, giving it a capability to handle all the cargo, passenger and fishing needs of the Solomon Islands.

The economy of the Solomons has remained primarily subsistence agriculture, with the country, overall, running a trade deficit. Tropical cyclones have not helped their cause, with several of disastrous proportions occurring in recent years. Tourism, as small as it is, has been an important source of income, especially so during the 50th anniversary of the Battle of Guadalcanal.

A shortsighted tourist industry let slip through the country's hands an irreplaceable attraction—the unique relics of World War II. Some of World War II's artifacts have been gathered together at places like the Vilu War Museum and Cemetery between Tassafaronga and Cape Esperance. Parts of airplanes, tanks, field guns and other relics have been collected in a crude outdoor display to show to the few visitors who get that far west on the island.

Honiara has tried in other ways to keep pace with the rest of the world in preserving and displaying its culture in a downtown museum. It also has a fine botanical garden providing a nice slice of nature's magnificent tropical environment. Flowers grow in profusion and multitudes of colorful butterflies flit gracefully about its tropical forest. Ironically, it is located in the same valley and ridge where the bitter November 1942 fighting took place.

The Solomons are often called the Happy Isles, for good reason. One cannot help but like the modern-day islanders, with red hibiscus in their hair and broad smiles on their faces, who, a half century ago, were unknown except to copra traders and beachcombers.

CHAPTER 5

TARAWA
A Place in History

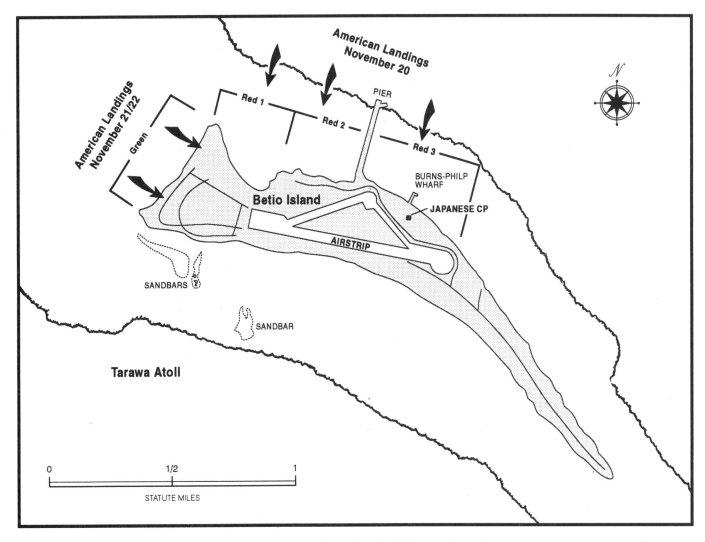

U.S. Operation GALVANIC - Tarawa Invasion

In August 1943 a drama took place in the central Pacific that was to reshape World War II. It happened on a minuscule bit of land, but it was to be a steppingstone of monumental proportions for the rest of the war.

Tarawa atoll, Gilbert Islands, was to be the proving ground for an untested American doctrine of amphibious landings needed in the Pacific. While the casualty toll was high, the operation paid off handsomely in later landings made right up to Japan's doorstep island of Okinawa.

Operation Galvanic was the code name for the invasion of Tarawa. This sleepy little paradisiacal atoll in the mid-Pacific had no reason for its coming notoriety except that the Japanese Imperial Navy captured it on Dec. 24, 1941, and

heavily fortified one little island. The Gilbert Islands became Japan's most remote outpost, but not for long.

A Concentrated Target

Betio (bay-sho), a tiny half-square-mile islet at Tarawa's southwest corner, was selected as the fortress. It was near the lagoon's only entrance and surrounded by coral reefs. A less hospitable place for amphibious landings could not be imagined. And the defensive works were the epitome of Japan's military engineering.

Steel-reinforced concrete up to six feet thick buttressed with coconut logs and coral sand was the material of choice

At the height of the bloody battle for Tarawa, a pillbox on Betio is taken with a frontal assault by U.S. Marines. This may be one of the Japanese bombproof shelters between Red Beach 1 and Red Beach 2 that were taken on November 23, 1943, after holding out for nearly the full 76 hours of the attack.

for command posts, pillboxes, bunkers and blockhouses. The island was surrounded by a continuous five-foot-high seawall made alternately of coral blocks and coconut logs to always give the defenders the high ground and deny the attackers a clear plain.

These defensive positions literally bristled with armament: 8-inch Vickers guns captured at Singapore; 80mm and 140mm antiboat guns; a variety of 37mm and 75mm field pieces; light tanks, machine guns, rifles and assorted small arms.

Manning these fortifications and weapons under Admiral Shibasaki were 2,619 garrison troops drawn from Japan's elite Special Naval Landing Forces. Backing them up were 2,217 construction workers, mostly Korean. They were well prepared to defend this tiny piece of sand against all but the most determined forces. The Japanese commandant boasted: "A million men cannot take Tarawa in a hundred years." But 5,600 Marines took it in three days and only 17 Japanese survived.

U.S. intelligence had determined that Betio was not intended as an offensive base for further Japanese conquest and it could really have been bypassed. But it had an airfield and lay within 350 miles of the Marshall Islands, which was the next stop on the road to Japan. With the Marshall inva-

sion set for late January 1944, the Tarawa event was set to begin on Nov. 20, 1943. The date proved calamitous.

The Coral Reef Problem

British advisers to Galvanic, who were familiar with the hydrography of the Gilberts, argued against that date. They pointed out that the moon was then in its last quarter, producing an unusually low and narrow range of tides. The advisers predicted only three feet of water over the reef flats, while Navy experts calculated five feet. Since a loaded Higgins landing boat draws only four feet, the Navy felt the margin with their numbers was safe.

But coral reefs do not grow at a single level and the need for boats to pick a route through raised coral heads was unfamiliar to Navy planners. The task force commander rejected the British adviser's argument. Operation Galvanic was ordered to proceed.

The softening-up bombardment of Betio began with long-range bomber raids from the Ellice Islands and Canton Island. Then came carrier aircraft to add more destruction. At 0440 on D-day, the battleships took up the bombardment while the first assault elements of the 2nd Marine Division

A Japanese tank and three Marine LVTs litter a Betio beach where they were destroyed during the invasion. Low tide reveals a panoply of material destruction.

under Gen. Julian Smith boarded landing craft a full five miles out at sea.

The Japanese defenders soon realized from the bombardment pattern that the landings would take place on the lagoon side of the island instead of over the south barrier reef for which they were well prepared. During lulls in the preinvasion bombardment, they quickly moved mobile weapons across the island and retrained their big guns. They knew this was going to be a battle to the death and the sons of the Rising Sun were going to give it everything they had.

A Poor Start

Beaches Red inside the lagoon were the sites of the initial landings by the Marines. Amphibious tractors (amphtracs) carried the first assault troops up onto the reef and crawled toward the shoreline in spite of the shallow water.

The defenders withheld their fire until the amphtracs were within 100 yards of the beach and then they opened a devastating fire.

With guts, luck and plenty of casualties the first Marine wave made it to the shoreline only to be confronted by the coconut-log barrier. That's when they found out that the amph-

tracs could not climb five-foot-high barricades. The assault force was pinned down on a 10-foot-wide strip of beach.

The attrition of the amphtracs in the three-day assault was high: 90 of the 125 amphtracs would be lost. The bulk of the landing forces that followed the amphtracs came ashore in Higgins boats, which grounded on the reef 700 yards from the beach. The Marines had to wade ashore under a withering fire, a lethal result of a flawed command decision.

Sherman tanks came later on even larger landing craft and they would do no better. They, too, had to traverse the wide reef under heavy fire from shore batteries. It was only the innate courage of the Marines that enabled enough men and equipment to get ashore to secure the beachhead for larger forces yet to come.

Heavy landing casualties over the reef and the very effective coconut-log barricade kept the attackers pinned down on Beaches Red. A reserve battalion was called in to reinforce them, but it, too, suffered the consequences of low tide and strong defense.

Late in the afternoon the struggling Marines managed to surmount the barricade at one point and set up a command post next to a wrecked pillbox. Other Marines also found their way over the barricade and had moved inland by night-

The northwestern corner of Betio Island, Tarawa, on Nov. 22, 1943 (D-day+2) after heavy bombardment and fighting. Red Beach 1 is to the left of the point and Green Beach is to the right. Several Marine LVTs (amphtracs) and a Japanese landing craft are on the beach, and several coastal defense guns, including two Vickers 8-inchers, are visible on the far shoreline (top of picture).

fall. Food, water and medical help were scarce and casualties continued to mount.

Additional landings made at dawn on the second day also were vigorously opposed by defenders who had worked all night to regroup men and equipment. With the freshly landed troops, however, came a renewed spirit, and the invasion momentum returned. Engineers began to methodically obliterate pillboxes, command posts and bunkers. By nightfall of Day 2, landings had also been made at Beach Green, and the island had been cut in two.

Success Appears Possible

The third day found the Marines in full control of their invasion, advancing down the island to occupy more than half of it by nightfall. Casualties continued heavy. The defenders made three banzai charges during the night, but all were thrown back. The third charge had been made with tradition-

al banzai weapons—bayonets and swords. It was a meaningful tactic only in a suicidal sense.

Seventy-six hours after the first landings, American forces were in control of Betio. It took two more days to clear the atoll's other islets of Japanese fanatics. The last battle was fought at Buariki village in north Tarawa.

Casualties were heavy on both sides. The defenders lost 4,690 men; the attackers had 1,072 dead or missing plus another 2,162 wounded. The innocent little island lost all of its top-hamper and inherited tons of useless iron, steel and concrete and an enduring reputation for what can happen when the irresistible force meets the immovable object.

Looking back 50 years, one 66-year-old Gilbertese said, "No one knew that the Americans were coming. They bombarded Betio from 6 p.m. till the next morning. Women and children escaped across the passage and sought shelter at Bairiki. Betio the next morning was a complete mess with no trees. When the U.S. Marines landed, they bravely managed

Members of a General Sherman tank unit sit atop their stalled vehicle in a shell hole in the Tarawa lagoon. Amphtracs are seen in the background continuing their shuttle delivery of men and supplies to the Betio shoreline.

Japanese aircraft revetments along the northwestern diagonal taxiway on Nov. 22, 1943. Heavy shellfire and bombs have demolished a barracks at right center and wrecked one of the revetments. A standard Japanese island latrine on stilts over the water is at the top center of the photo.

to penetrate through well-fortified Betio."

In the aftermath of that terrible 76 hours, the Americans retired back to Hawaii to gird their loins for yet other landings to come. The few Japanese and Korean prisoners went into prison camps for the duration, and the Gilbertese, who had wisely retreated to the other islets, returned to the southern islands to pick up their lives.

A New Nation Arises

Before World War II and until 1979, the Gilbert Islands were part of the British Gilbert and Ellice Islands Colony. At independence in 1979, the Gilbert Islands were amalgamated with the Phoenix and Line Islands to become the Republic of Kiribati (keeribas). From a subsistence economy badly shaken by 76 hours of hellfire on Betio, Kiribati has gamely fought to enter the modern world as a country whose resources are 1 million square miles of ocean, 33 coral atolls and a burgeoning population of nearly 70,000.

Today, Tarawa has problems similar to those of other Pacific atolls—overpopulation combined with a lack of water, jobs and housing. Betio has become the shipping center, and adjacent Bairiki, which figured in the battle only as the escape hope for the few Japanese who made it across the two-mile sand spit, is now the government, business and financial center.

Remnants of World War II still occupy prominent positions on Betio. Reinforced concrete structures do not disintegrate on their own and the sturdy Japanese command posts, bunkers and pillboxes stand as silent monuments to the 76-hour holocaust.

The big guns from Singapore rust away in the hot sun of this equatorial island. The fringing reef in front of Beaches Red is still home to shells of Sherman tanks, while a few amphtrac skeletons lie aimlessly on the beach.

Hawkins Airfield, the real plum in the invasion, has been divided and subdivided for housing, stores, storage yards and water tanks, its runway and taxiways hardly distinguishable in places. It has been replaced as Tarawa's airport by a jetport at the southeastern corner of the atoll.

The current population knows little about the ferocity of the battle. The few who witnessed it on the outer islands are passing into oblivion. Second-, third- and fourth-generation Gilbertese live, work and play among the remnants of battle with little feeling for history. Operation Galvanic? They will have to read about it in books.

CHAPTER 6

MARSHALL ISLANDS
A Practical Strategy

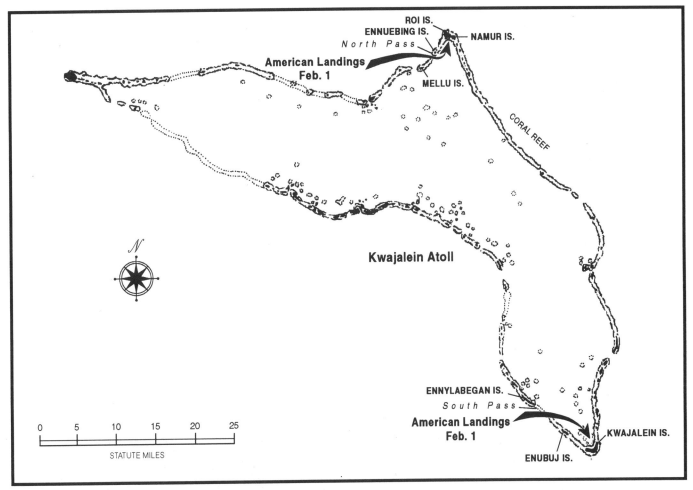

ROI IS.
ENNUEBING IS.
NAMUR IS.
North Pass
American Landings
Feb. 1
MELLU IS.
CORAL REEF
Kwajalein Atoll
ENNYLABEGAN IS.
South Pass
American Landings
Feb. 1
KWAJALEIN IS.
ENUBUJ IS.

0 5 10 15 20 25
STATUTE MILES

U.S. Operation FLINTLOCK - Kwajalein Invasion

Japan's occupation of the Marshall Islands dated back to 1914, when it took over from the Germans at the beginning of World War I. Although the League of Nations mandate, which gave Japan the islands, said they were not to be fortified, the Japanese withdrew from the League in 1935 and, from that time on, the outside world suspected that the islands were being fortified. Japan effectively kept foreigners out, and the extent of fortifications was unverifiable.

After the Japanese southward expansion was stopped at Guadalcanal and New Guinea, Admiral Nimitz contended that the best path to Japan was through the central Pacific.

There were, however, two barriers to overcome—the Marshall and Truk Islands. Intelligence estimates indicated that both island groups were heavily defended. But with the capture of Tarawa and Makin in November 1943, American forces had obtained good air bases within range of Truk and the Marshalls, which were still called by the Japanese "unsinkable aircraft carriers"—but unmaneuverable, also.

Aerial reconnaissance flights from the Gilberts started Dec. 4, 1943. These, supplemented by submarine reports, showed that the atolls of Kwajalein, Jaluit, Mili, Wotje, Maloelap and Eniwetok had airfields and shore defenses. As was to be learned later, though, none of the island defenses came close to being as formidable as those on Tarawa. Reasons were they were started later and the quality of cement used was poor.

While some tactical planners thought the attack on the Marshalls should be made against the eastern atolls first, Admiral Nimitz took the position that American forces should concentrate on Kwajalein, which was the known hub

Left: American soldiers of the Army's 7th Infantry Division, with rifles and bayonets ready, wait as a flame thrower is used to flush out Japanese defenders in a blockhouse on Kwajalein Island. Hand-to-hand combat was common in the Marshalls campaign.

Bottom: Pfc N.E. Carling stands beside the medium tank named "Killer" on which is carried a Japanese light tank "captured" on Kwajalein Atoll, Feb. 2, 1944.

A rare Japanese prisoner, sitting on the ground, is questioned by an officer as men of the 4th Marine Division keep an eye on him and the enemy fortification beyond in the smoking debris during fighting on Namur Island.

of enemy military activities. They would attack Kwajalein Island, the largest of the islands making up the atoll, and the Siamese-twin islands of Roi-Namur in the atoll first while holding the enemy at bay on the other islands with air and sea bombardment. A later assault on Eniwetok would round out Operation Flintlock/Catchpole.

Kwajalein Island Seized

Preliminary to the landings on Kwajalein by the Army 7th Infantry Division, two small islands to the northwest, Ennylabegan and Enubui, were captured on D-day, Jan. 31, 1944. They bordered the main pass into the southern end of the atoll. Their role was destined to be that of a supply dump, a repair station and an emplacement for offensive artillery. Both islands were secured by noon and artillery was landed and in position by 1500, when registration fire on Kwajalein was begun.

Landing conditions on the west end of Kwajalein were given a final inspection by Army and Navy underwater demolition teams (UDTs) sent ashore in rubber boats under cover of battleship fire. Their mission was to locate wrecks, coral heads and underwater obstructions that could delay the next day's landings. This was the first time in the Pacific that the UDTs were deployed, and it reflected a bitter lesson learned at Tarawa.

The assault landings against the western end of Kwajalein began at 0930 on D-day+1 following an unprecedented sea and air bombardment. Troops of the 7th Division

under Gen. Charles Corlett were landed that day with little resistance, and by nightfall, the western one-quarter of the island had been taken. Defenses stiffened on D-day+2, and tank movement was temporarily halted by a tank trap backed up by pillboxes. An end run around the trap via the ocean beach put tanks behind the trap, and they eliminated the pillboxes allowing forward movement once again.

On D-day+3, the compacting of the enemy into the narrow eastern end of the island, which had an increased number of pillboxes and other defenses, gave the enemy a great defensive advantage. This slowed the attack and it wasn't until the morning of D-day+4 that the final push to the east end was successfully made. Securing the 2-mile-long island had taken longer than expected because of the extensive underground defenses and the tenacity of the defenders.

The Battle of Roi-Namur

The 4th Marine Division, under Gen. Harry Schmidt, launched its attack against Roi-Namur in the northeast corner of the atoll on the same time schedule and in the same manner as at Kwajalein Island. Photo-reconnaissance flights had shown Roi to have an active airfield and light ground defenses. Adjacent Namur was heavily wooded, and there was evidence of stronger ground defenses.

The neighboring islands of Enneubing and Mellu on the southwest flank of Roi-Namur adjacent to the passes of the same names were only lightly defended and were quickly overrun by the Marines on D-day. Howitzers were landed on

An American plane sweeps over Eniwetok Atoll to strafe the enemy in their coral trenches, while a group of Marines lies prone in the sand peppering the Japanese with rifle and machine-gun fire across a smoking no-man's-land.

these islands to take up the bombardment of Roi-Namur. Then the three small islands on Roi-Namur's opposite flank were seized, but many defenders escaped to Namur by wading across the reef between islands.

Roi and Namur were attacked the morning of D-day+1. Marines landed at lagoon beaches, which were known to be the soft underbellies of the islands. Although blockhouses and 127mm guns defended the ocean side of the islands, nothing more than pillboxes and a few 20mm antiaircraft guns protected the lagoon beaches.

There were, however, some 3,000 fanatical Japanese defenders to resist the invasion. The airfield island of Roi was subdued by nightfall of the first day.

Namur was far better fortified than Roi, and it took another 18 hours of hand-to-hand combat to secure it. A major deterrent was the explosion of a large torpedo warhead magazine, which sent smoke and debris 1,000 feet into the

air and resulted in the death of 20 Marines. Not until the following morning of D-day+2, after the cause of the violent explosions had been determined, did the American advance continue. By noon, the entire island was secure.

It took another two days to completely mop up the Japanese defenders on all 97 islets composing Kwajalein, the world's largest atoll. The tactics used to subdue Kwajalein were a great improvement over those used at Tarawa.

Eniwetok Is Taken

After the easy capture of Kwajalein, the date for Operation Catchpole, the seizing of Eniwetok, was moved ahead to February 17. But one other action had to be taken first to ensure success and that was the neutralization of Truk, which could send enemy aircraft against the Eniwetok invasion fleet.

The initial neutralization of Truk by carrier aircraft took

Marines advance under fire at Red Beach 1 on Roi Island to capture the airport island in a swift one-day campaign invasion.

Palm-studded Carlos Island in Kwajalein Atoll becomes a "Paradise Lost" to the Japanese defenders as American invasion forces are driven ashore in a Coast Guard landing craft.

place on February 17 and 18 and continued throughout the rest of the war. Truk was never invaded. (See "Truk—'Gibraltar of the Pacific' Neutralized," Chapter 10.)

Prime targets in Eniwetok were Engebi, Parry and Eniwetok islands, which intelligence had learned harbored effective defense personnel. Parry held the largest garrison. The effectiveness of all of the garrisons was, however, severe-ly reduced by American air strikes that damaged installa-tions, destroyed weapons, ammunition and foodstuffs and inflicted numerous casualties.

With assurance that there would be no enemy aircraft interference from Truk, the Eniwetok Expeditionary Group, under Adm. Harry Hill, arrived off the atoll the morning of February 17. The islands of Engebi, Eniwetok and Parry were invaded in that order, and all were secured by sundown on D-day+3.

Collectively, the American casualties in the Marshalls campaign were 3,281, of which 915 were killed or missing in action. Japanese casualties amounted to 11,910 troops and support personnel killed or committed suicide. Only 363 Japanese and Korean personnel surrendered.

American ship, airplane and equipment losses were minimal due to better tactics, better equipment and the neutralization of enemy air power. Fire-support battleships in the Marshalls campaign moved to within an unprecedented 2,000 yards of their targets to deliver pinpoint fire. Experience from the earlier campaigns was now proving its worth.

The Marshalls Today

After years of benign neglect as a ward of the United States Trusteeship of the Pacific Islands, the Republic of the Marshall Islands came into being in 1986 as a self-ruling country in "free association" with the United States. The Republic's capital is on Majuro, which has a population of 20,000. The second most populated island is Ebeye, with a population in excess of 9,000.

Ebeye Island's 76 acres has become the bedroom community for support workers at the U.S. Army's Strategic Defense Test Base on Kwajalein. The extended families of Marshallese having well-paying jobs on Kwajalein moved from the outer islands to Ebeye to share in their relatives' good fortune. This turned the island into a slum. Both the Marshall Islands government and the Army have been trying to improve living conditions, but progress is slow.

Life today in the Marshall Islands is a mixture of high tech at Kwajalein, traditional life in the outer islands and a muddled western culture in Majuro. All the ills of western civilization are present, such as alcoholism, TV, fast foods and unemployment. Much of the Marshallese problem has to do with overpopulation brought on by a high birthrate, almost the highest in the world.

Soon after the war ended, Bikini and Eniwetok residents, as well as some from other atolls, were displaced to make room for the postwar nuclear bomb tests the United States conducted there. After a massive cleanup, the islanders were allowed to return only to Eniwetok Island in 1980. Displaced islanders are impatiently awaiting the time when they can return home to nuclear-free islands. Nuclear radiation being what it is, the wait may be long.

The Marshallese, who have lived a traditional subsistence life heretofore, are having a hard time assimilating the trappings of the Western world. Maybe their lot was better before the Germans, Japanese and Americans arrived.

CHAPTER 7

RABAUL
Bypassed Fortress Neutralized by Airpower

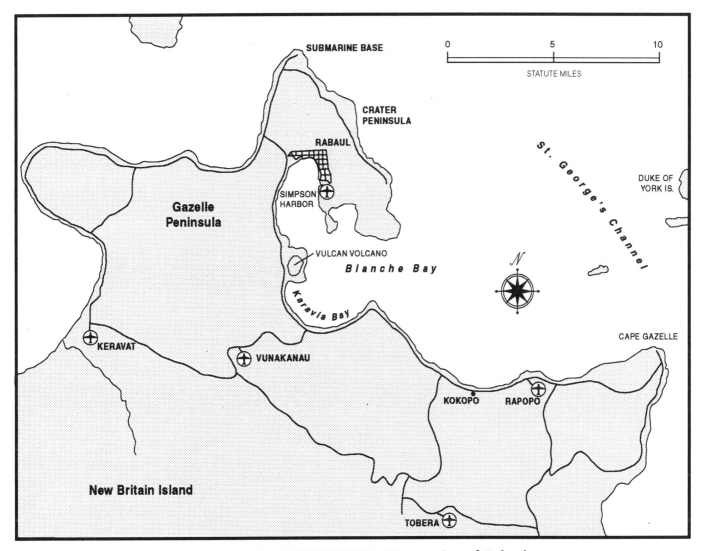

U.S. Operation CARTWHEEL - Destruction of Rabaul

Rabaul township on New Britain Island has had a long history of violence. It was built on the site of an ancient caldera, which, as recently as 1,400 years ago, suffered a major explosion opening one side of it to ocean waters and creating one of the South Pacific's finest harbors. Seismic disturbances, both large and small, have continued to this day, reshaping the Gazelle peninsula of New Britain.

As if nature's violence was not enough pain to bear, the indigenous Tolai people were exploited economically by the Germans at the turn of the century and then by the Australians under a League of Nations Mandate at the start of World War I. But they didn't bargain for the large Japanese naval force that landed at Rabaul on Jan. 23, 1942, easily overwhelming the small Australian garrison.

Rabaul offered great strategic value to Japan's World War II drive into the southwest Pacific. It was only 440 miles from New Guinea, their planned steppingstone to control that island, and 565 miles from Guadalcanal, their outpost intended to cut Allied shipping routes to Australia. They, in fact, occupied the entire Bismarck Archipelago in May 1942 as a protective measure, making the outlook bleak for the Allies.

New Zealand and Australia had already deployed large numbers of their troops and equipment to Europe to combat Hitler's aggression. America was still thousands of miles

A Grumman F6F Hellcat fighter descends on the elevator to the hangar deck of the carrier Saratoga *after a raid on Rabaul. Other Hellcats are maneuvered into position on the flight deck preparatory to launching another raid.*

An Army North American B-25 Mitchell medium bomber makes a low-altitude bomb run over a Japanese cargo ship in Simpson Harbor in late 1943 as other ships and shore facilities burn along Rabaul's waterfront.

away and its sea and air power had been seriously hurt by the infamous Pearl Harbor blow. Nevertheless, the Japanese juggernaut had to be stopped at any cost before it proceeded farther south.

The opportunity came as the result of the Japanese miscalculation in attempting the invasion of Midway in the North Pacific. Their disastrous defeat there had cost them four irre-

placeable aircraft carriers and hundreds of first-line aircraft and pilots. That loss put a damper on other Pacific operations, enough to allow the Allies to mount counterattacks in the southwest Pacific, thereby halting the Japanese drive.

The Allies' southwest Pacific war plan had been conceived to 1) stop the advancing enemy in New Guinea and drive him back up the northeastern coast, 2) recapture Tulagi

Incendiary bombing by U.S. Army planes of a Japanese airfield on the plateau southwest of Rabaul.

and Guadalcanal in the Solomon Islands and 3) seize and occupy Rabaul on New Britain.

The forces available to throw against the Japanese in early 1942 were a combination of American, Australian and New Zealand troops, ships and planes. Logistics support was tenuous at best, for America was still committed to a European Theater priority, and the supply line to the South Pacific was thousands of miles long. Hit-and-run tactics were employed at first by the U.S. carrier task forces to make their presence felt in the area. By Feb. 21, 1942, the planes of the Lexington had made their first strike against Rabaul.

Japanese High Command Entrenched

Rabaul had, by this time, become a major Japanese military installation. Its magnificent Simpson Harbor was filled with cargo vessels bringing in supplies and troops. Airfields had been built on surrounding plateaus, and liberal antiaircraft defenses were placed around the harbor.

Tens of thousands of troops were deployed over New Britain, while the Japanese high command was installed in reinforced concrete bunkers in Rabaul to direct their southwest Pacific operations. All of this was well known to the Allies through aerial and submarine reconnaissance. The Japanese base at Rabaul had to be eliminated if Allied forces were to proceed northwestward to the Philippines.

Due north of Rabaul, a distance of 700 miles, were the

Truk Islands, described at that time as the Japanese "Gibraltar of the Pacific." This was the staging area for ships, aircraft, troops and supplies destined for Rabaul and Japan's southwest Pacific campaign. In charge of this extensive Pacific operation was Adm. Isoroku Yamamoto. No story of the Rabaul campaign would be complete without a retelling of the bizarre end of this capable admiral.

The Japanese air forces were suffering severe setbacks in trying to control the air over the northern Solomon Islands. Yamamoto decided in March 1943 to step in and take a hand at beating the Allied air forces. He left his Truk headquarters and, bringing with him a number of carrier aircraft squadrons, set up headquarters in Rabaul.

Judging from grossly exaggerated reports by his fliers, he thought he had succeeded in blunting the Allied air forces in New Guinea and the Solomons by April. He ordered his carrier planes back to Truk and scheduled himself on a morale-building flight to visit the troops at Buin island.

But the overly optimistic reports on Allied air power losses were to be his end. Learning of his visit, the 13th Army Air Force sent a flight of P-38 fighters from Guadalcanal to wait in ambush for his arrival.

The punctilious Yamamoto's two bomber-transports arrived on time and were sitting ducks for the P-38s. Yamamoto perished in the downing of the planes, and the Japanese southwest Pacific campaign suffered yet another irreplaceable loss.

Japanese ships attempt to maneuver out of harm's way during an Army bombing raid on Rabaul on Nov. 5, 1943. At upper left is Matupit-Greet Harbor.

The Japanese offensive on New Guinea itself was in full swing in early 1943. A reinforcement convoy of eight troop transports escorted by destroyers departed Rabaul in February headed for Lae, New Guinea. Japanese air power from Rabaul was to provide air cover, but it failed to stop the Allied planes, which totally decimated the naval force, with tremendous loss of Japanese ships and lives. This was the Battle of the Bismarck Sea. It was a big victory for the Allies, but further convinced them of the necessity of neutralizing Rabaul as a support base.

Allies Target Rabaul

About this time the Allies instituted Operation Cartwheel—the reduction of Rabaul. Rabaul's four airfields at Tobera, Vunakanau, Rapopo and Keravat were thorns in the side of the Allied movements as was Rabaul's naval ship support.

To neutralize these bases, the Allies first had to get close enough to Rabaul to make an attack, and the only way to do that was to move up the heavily defended northeast coast of New Guinea and up through the Solomon Islands.

The climate and topography of all of these islands were enemies in themselves. Rain fell regularly. Trails became morasses of mud, bogging down soldiers and vehicles alike. Supplies had to be air-dropped to forward units. The sodden, humid heat took its toll of ground troops. Malaria, skin fungus, infections and plain exhaustion incapacitated large numbers of ground troops, but they persevered.

The northwestward Allied advance under Gen. MacArthur continued up the New Guinea coast with operations at Salamaua, Markham Valley, Nadzab, Lae and Finschafen. Concurrently, advances by troops under Adm. William Halsey were made up the Solomons through Choiseul, Treasury and Bougainville islands. Eventually this two-pronged advance would link up in the Bismarck Islands.

By late 1943 Rabaul had been virtually surrounded. Allied air bases were within short range on all sides and the U.S. 5th Air Force, flying medium and heavy bombers, pounded Rabaul at will. It became so intense that on Nov. 12, 1943, Japan withdrew all of its carrier planes and cruisers from Rabaul assuring the end of any offensive capability from this base, but the Japanese were not to give up entirely.

The town of Rabaul is subjected to an intense aerial bombardment on Mar. 22, 1944. Street patterns and bomb craters meld in one destructive aerial orgy. Ships were untargeted.

In December they literally went underground, building 360 miles of tunnels in the Gazelle Peninsula to gain shelter from the ceaseless uncontested air attacks by the Allies. They built living quarters, hospitals, supply storage, ammunition dumps, and combat bunkers to defend against an expected enemy invasion—one that was never to come. At the eastern tip of the peninsula was the "submarine base," so called because the sheer 300-meter coral face of the island at this point allowed supply submarines to come right up to the base of the cliff and unload supplies directly into nearby tunnels. The mighty Japanese base of Rabaul may have become an impotent offensive base, but it still had defensive value.

Rather than waste men and materiel on invading Rabaul, the Allies chose to bypass it and continued island hopping to the north to the Admiralty Islands. The Japanese played their last battle card of the Solomon Islands campaign with an ill-fated attempt to dislodge U.S. Army troops from Empress Augusta Bay. This effectively ended the southwest Pacific campaign in March 1944. Fortress Rabaul, with 100,000 Japanese troops still in nearby camps, as well as the heavily defended base at Kavieng, New Ireland, was

left to wither on the vine until the end of the Pacific War.

The Fruits of Peace

At war's end in 1945, the United Nations established New Guinea as a trust territory under Australian administration and it became the independent country of Papua New Guinea in 1975. The years of foreign rule and war devastation had come to an end. It was time for a new generation of New Guineans to bring their war-torn country into the 20th century. Rabaul town took its place as the capital of the East New Britain province.

Until the most recent volcanic eruptions, Rabaul was a colorful town of 40,000 persons lying on the shores of beautiful Simpson Harbor. The streets were lined with trees and exotic flora that only the tropics can grow. The rich volcanic soil has always produced an abundance of fruits and vegetables for local consumption as well as export. The primary industry outside of agriculture has been tourism, for its history, its people and its geography are of exciting interest to visitors. World War II relics are to be found in the bush, especially near the old airfields. The floor of Simpson Harbor is a treasure trove of sunken ships. The hills contain the abandoned network of tunnels, and scuba diving is fantastic off the "submarine base."

Life would be a perfect tropical paradise except for the volcanoes surrounding Simpson Harbor. There have been several serious eruptions over the past three centuries, the most recent occurring in September 1994. Constant tremors remind everyone in Rabaul that the earth beneath them is still alive and that Rabaul and Simpson Harbor may not yet have assumed their final form. On signal from the Rabaul Volcanological Observatory (much of whose equipment and many of whose procedures were developed by the Japanese), the entire population will evacuate, as they did in 1994, never sure they will return and be able to rebuild their city to its former glory. Indeed, it was announced after the 1994 disaster that, except for the main wharf and associated commercial structures, the city would be rebuilt at a new location some 50 km (31 mi.) away.

CHAPTER 8

NEW GUINEA
Foundation for Closing the Ring

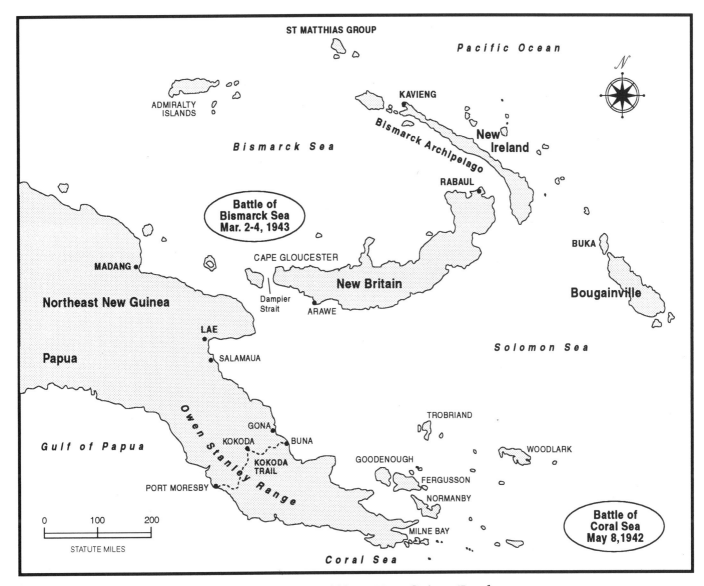

U.S. Operation ELKTON - New Guinea Retaken

The Japanese planned the southernmost perimeter of their Greater East Asia Co-Prosperity Sphere to stop short of Australia. One reason was they did not have enough soldiers to occupy it. But they would invade and hold Port Moresby, just 300 miles across the Torres Straits from Australia's Cape York Peninsula, to intimidate Australia and protect its newly captured islands. It was their mistaken belief that Australia would not be of a mind to continue the war if their homeland was not directly threatened. Port Moresby would be the buffer between them.

Japanese forces moved south from Truk on Jan. 23, 1942, with little opposition, spreading out and occupying the entire Bismarck Archipelago by May. Occupation of the archipelago essentially isolated the Solomon Islands from New Guinea, seemingly to prevent the Allies from using them against each other. Little did Japan realize that this strategy would backfire later when the Allies would reverse the procedure and use both the Solomons and New Guinea as pincers to throttle the life out of Rabaul, which was by then the main Japanese naval and air base in the southwest Pacific.

The Japanese war machine moved swiftly and with precise timing from Rabaul to occupy strategic coastal villages along the north coast of New Guinea—Hollandia, Wewak, Madang, Lae and Salamaua. They chased out scattered Dutch and Australian forces with ease.

Occupation of these new bases was the precursor to securing the southern rim of their Greater East Asia Co-Prosperity Sphere[1]. To complete the defensive line, Japan prepared to obtain the requisite bases on the southern coast of New Guinea. In planning this offensive, to be called "Operation MO" (for Moresby), they failed to recognize the natural barrier to military operations presented by this primeval island.

New Guinea is the second largest island in the world, after Greenland. It measures 1,500 miles long and is 500 miles across at its widest. Lying just a few degrees south of the equator, New Guinea is hot, wet and pestilential. It was an almost impenetrable jungle in 1942 and is not much different today. There are great outcroppings of mountains to heights of almost 15,000 feet having precipitous slopes and knife-sharp ridges separated by broad, upland valleys at elevations up to 10,000 feet. These heights ramble down to lower rolling foothills, descending still farther onto coastal lowlands consisting mostly of riverine swamps of sago, bamboo, mosquitoes and leeches.

New Guinea entered modern history as a pawn of the Dutch, British and German Pacific empires. Dutch New Guinea was the entire western half of the island pointing directly into the seven seas of the Dutch East Indies.

The eastern half of the island of New Guinea was divided by a gentleman's treaty giving Germany the northern half, simply called New Guinea, and Britain (represented by Australia) the southern half, called Papua. World War I later stripped Germany of any authority in New Guinea, and Australia became the sole surviving colonial power on the eastern half of the island until its invasion by Japanese forces in World War II.

---

[1] Japan's Greater East Asia Co-Prosperity Sphere (see map page viii) was composed of three geographic elements, in addition to the home islands: (1) those Pacific islands received as mandates from the League of Nations after World War I; (2) the countries of the Asian mainland they had conquered in their aggressions of the 1930s; and (3) the additional Asian countries and Pacific islands they were taking at the outset of World War II. "Asia for the Asiatics" was their argument for this "new order."

The Asian lands were wanted for agricultural and manufacturing needs as well as for population expansion. The islands to the south were needed for their petroleum reserves. The remaining Pacific islands were to form a defensive perimeter. It was their belief that by quickly acquiring these lands, they could sue for a negotiated peace with the non-warlike nations on their new borders. This would assure domination over their grandiose Greater East Asia Co-Prosperity Sphere.

The idea that the rest of the world would not strongly oppose their actions seemingly sprang from an inherited isolationist thinking. By keeping aloof from the rest of the world during their entire history, they failed to understand that other countries were just as protective of their lands and that they would take up arms, however belatedly, and defend themselves. Thus, Japan's Co-Prosperity Sphere was doomed from the start.

The Yanks mop up on Bougainville. At night the Japanese infiltrated the American lines, and at dawn the GIs sought them out in a dangerous game of hide and seek. Infantrymen often followed closely on the tracks of a tank to do this.

A Failed End-Around Play

Japan assembled its invasion group in Rabaul, intending to steam around the east end of New Guinea and approach Port Moresby from the south. This invasion group, under Admiral Goto, included the light carrier *Shoho*. On May 4, the Japanese invasion force left Rabaul, and the supporting carrier force under Admiral Hara and including the large carriers *Shokaku* and *Zuikaku* met it at sea.

Receiving word of the ship movements from Australian aerial reconnaissance and coastwatchers, newly appointed U.S. Pacific commander Adm. Chester Nimitz directed Adm. Frank Fletcher's Task Force 17, including the carriers *Lexington* and *Yorktown*, toward the Coral Sea. There it could intercept the Japanese invasion force.

For several days the forces of both sides jockeyed for position based on unreliable and constantly changing intelli-

gence. On May 8, 1942, they finally locked horns in what became the Battle of the Coral Sea. The battle raged on and off for two days as each side located additional ship targets spread over hundreds of miles of open sea. It was the first naval battle in history in which opposing fleets did not see each other. The encounters were totally dependent on aircraft strikes.

The results of the battle were indecisive, that is, except for the faulty Japanese belief that they had sunk both *Saratoga* (it was actually *Lexington* that was sunk) and *Yorktown* that was later to prove their nemesis at Midway. The Japanese lost only the light carrier *Shoho*. Japan's propaganda machine made a great victory of it and the empire from the Coral Sea to Tokyo chose to believe continuing overly optimistic battle reports setting the stage for disaster in a later attempt to destroy the U.S. fleet at Midway.

While some experts considered this Battle of the Coral

Left: U.S. Marine Raiders gathered in front of a Japanese dugout on Cape Totkina on Bougainville, Solomon Islands. The Raiders earned the reputation of being skillful jungle fighters.

Bottom: Army Signal Corps cameramen Sgt. Carl Weinke and Pfc Ernest Marjoram wade across a jungle stream while following troops that had just landed on Beach Red 2 at Tanahmerah Bay on April 22, 1944. The role of the combat photographer was always a dangerous one.

Troops of the U.S. 41st Infantry Division hit the beach at Wakde Island in Dutch New Guinea on May 18, 1944, after earlier success at Aitape. Note hand grenade in sand, lower right.

Sea a draw, it marked the southernmost penetration of Japanese forces in World War II.

New Guinea the Battlefield

Australia and Port Moresby's eventual salvation came in the form of a new Allied supreme command in the southwest Pacific headed up by no less a military genius than Gen. Douglas MacArthur. He had been spirited out of the Philippines in March 1942 on President Roosevelt's order. His assignment was to halt the Japanese advance on Australia and then drive them back out of the South Pacific to allow the retaking of the Philippines.

This was a major task, considering that men and materials were still being given priority in the European Theater and that the U.S. Navy, not under his command, had its own assignment in the Solomons and the central Pacific.

Failure of the Japanese navy to capture Port Moresby after the Battle of the Coral Sea left it up to the Japanese army to cross the Owen Stanley Range and reach Port Moresby via a land route. But they did not reckon with Mother Nature, the new Allied commander and the now fighting-mad troops of Australia.

The crack Japanese South Seas Detachment was given the assignment to get to Port Moresby via the precipitous 100-mile-long Kokoda Trail over the unfriendly Owen

A Coast Guard-manned LST follows behind columns of troop-laden LCIs en route to the invasion of Cape Sansapor, New Guinea. The deck of the LST is closely packed with motorized fighting equipment.

Stanleys from Buna and Gona. Capturing Buna in July 1942, they started the difficult over-mountain thrust against Port Moresby.

A company of Australians, supported by a few hundred native militia, fought a delaying action against the Japanese as they ascended the Owen Stanleys. Additional Australian forces were on their way from Port Moresby, but by early September the Japanese forces had crossed the spine of the mountains and on September 18 they were within 35 miles of Port Moresby. They could see the lights of the harbor, but that was as close as they would get.

A tenuous 65-mile-long supply line over what probably was the world's worst terrain, a stubborn Australian defense force, intensive air bombing by the now organized 5th Army Air Force and the newly opened front on Guadalcanal robbed the men of the Japanese South Seas Detachment of their vitality and they withdrew back to the Buna coastline.

The Japanese, however, were not yet ready to accept defeat on New Guinea soil. They recognized the need for reinforcing their garrisons in the Salamaua-Lae area; in fact, they wanted to triple the forces by adding 6,900 soldiers held in reserve at the Rabaul staging area.

A convoy consisting of eight transports and eight destroyers was formed at Rabaul and sailed at midnight Feb. 28, 1943, under cover of an approaching storm. It was hoped that the storm plus fighter cover from Rabaul would protect the convoy from Allied air attack, but it didn't. Through a break in the clouds, a U.S. B-24 sighted the convoy and on March 2 heavy bombers of General Kenney's 5th Army Air Force struck, sinking one cargo vessel and damaging two others.

On March 3, the convoy had cleared Dampier Strait but was attacked by B-17s and B-25 bombers, the latter having just been equipped with eight .50-caliber nose gun batteries plus skip-bombing equipment. While Allied fighter cover held off a meager Japanese fighter force, the B-25s decimated the convoy. The little the Army planes missed was cleaned up by Navy motor torpedo boats. Of the 16 ships in the original convoy, only four destroyers escaped sinking.

This Battle of the Bismarck Sea (at least that was where it had started), with its heavy Japanese casualties, resulted in the loss of momentum and desire by the Japanese high command to pursue the eastern New Guinea offensive. From then on, they were on the defensive until finally driven by MacArthur's forces from the western tip of the Vogelkop of Dutch New Guinea in July 1944.

Allied Forces Drive North

The Australian and American push northwest along the shoreline of New Guinea began with Buna in November 1942 and continued west to the Vogelkop. It was one unbelievable patchwork of nonstop battles fought under the worst conditions of rain, mud, rushing rivers, malaria and dysentery, to say nothing of fanatical Japanese who, when in retreat, were always given the same order, "annihilate the enemy."

MacArthur chose to leapfrog many enemy positions as his troops moved west along the northern coast. Important battles would be fought by the 7th Australian Division and the 41st Army Division, supported by the 5th Army Air Force, initially to conquer Lae and Salamaua on New Guinea and then Arawe and Cape Gloucester across the Dampier Straits on New Britain.

American landings made farther west on mainland New Guinea at Siador in January 1944 bottled up thousands of Japanese soldiers and left such strongholds as Madang to die on the vine. A major goal in MacArthur's strategy was to reach far up the northern coast and capture Hollandia in Dutch New Guinea (now Jayapura in the Irian Jaya province of Indonesia). An invasion force put ashore at Hollandia in April 1944 was unopposed by the enemy, whose 11,000 personnel fled into the hills.

MacArthur's leapfrogging tactics gained speed and he immediately seized enemy airstrips 125 miles farther west from Hollandia at Maffin Bay and the important airfield on Wakde Island in May 1944. Two months later, American and Australian troops had leaped onto the Vogelkop, the western end of New Guinea, and that ended the formal part of the New Guinea campaign.

Soldiers left to mop up the area would dispute that the campaign ended so neatly since mopping-up operations would take many more months. At any rate, MacArthur was now ready to make good on his promise to return to the Philippines, for only Palau stood in his way and the U.S. Navy and Marines were scheduled to neutralize it.

40,000 Years of Progress

New Guinea today is still the hot, humid, sparsely settled island it always was. It is still divided—Indonesia claims the western (former Dutch) end as its province of Irian Jaya, while the eastern half has become the independent country of Papua New Guinea, including the islands of the Bismarck and Admiralty archipelagos.

But the fighting hasn't stopped. Both Indonesia and Papua New Guinea feel they should rule all of the main island, and border skirmishes are frequent. After all, it was at one time, one people. Or was it?

When European explorers discovered it, there were more than 700 different tribal cultures and they still seem to exist today. Unity had never been very important to the native, who spends most of his time simply keeping alive in the face of tropical disease, infertile land in many areas and internecine warfare.

While the Indonesians rule Irian Jaya with an iron fist and an almost closed society, Papua New Guinea has elected a democratic government that finds it a challenge to integrate the varied cultures of the tribes.

The mainland population of Papua New Guinea overwhelms the peoples of the Bismarck and Admiralty archipelagos, causing considerable political and economic friction. The island of Bougainville (geologically a northward extension of the Solomons), with its Bougainville Revolutionary Army, has been trying to separate from the parent nation and proceed on an independent path using the wealth of its copper mines to sustain it. Papua New Guinea armed forces have not been able to quell the inner desires of the separatists and the matter has not been resolved, although there have been talks in an effort to bring peace.

The copper of Bougainville has been a major source of trade dollars for Papua New Guinea over the years, but is on hold now. Oil was discovered in the 1980s and by mid-1992 it was being exported. Gold, the first mineral to be discovered, continues to be a source of revenue partially offsetting copper losses. There are few other natural resources except those that grow in the sun—coffee, copra, cocoa and spices. But massive price declines in recent years have caused the growers to seek urban employment.

The standard of living in all Papua New Guinea is low and unemployment high. Several towns, including Port Moresby, have a severe problem with crime, making tourism an iffy business.

Today, 60 percent of Papua New Guinea's business is controlled by Australians, a result of trade connections of long standing. Without that connection to the international economy, though, their total domestic economy would be in danger of reverting to a subsistence level.

The interior mountain ranges, to this day, are a barrier to road building and only the airplane and satellite communications tie the country together.

It is ironic that those nations who fought so hard to get control of New Guinea are all prospering while the people of Papua New Guinea struggle for survival. Like Air Niugini's in-flight magazine says: Papua New Guinea is "like no place you've ever been." Fifty years have made little difference in its 40,000 years of existence.

CHAPTER 9

NEW HEBRIDES
Supplying the War Machine

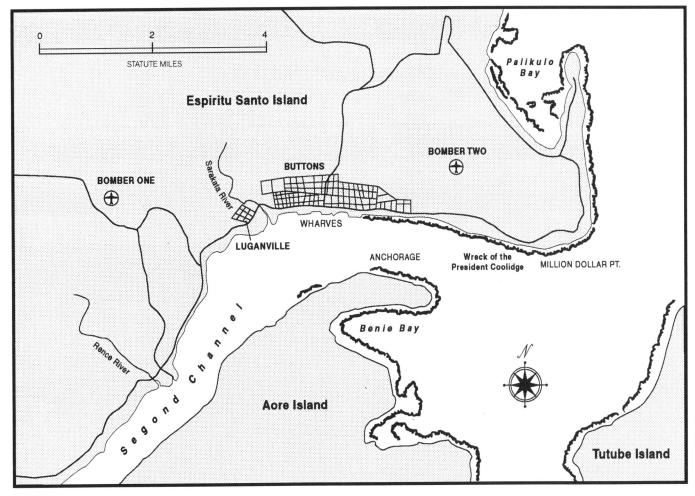

U.S. Staging Base BUTTONS - New Hebrides Islands

In the spring of 1942, the Allies were hard put to slow the southward advance of Japanese Imperial Forces through the Bismarck and Solomon island groups and along the eastern coast of New Guinea. The Japanese were planning on using these islands as steppingstones to their ultimate goal, the New Guinea mainland.

Allied troops and materials were in short supply down under because New Zealand and Australia already were embroiled in the war in Europe and to a large extent had drained their military resources dry. It was apparent that America would have to supply vast numbers of troops and supporting war materiel to fully stop the enemy and then drive him back out of the South Pacific.

But America was 5,000 miles away and its production might and manpower would have to be marshaled at loca-

tions convenient to the fighting fronts. General MacArthur and Admiral Nimitz gambled that the Japanese could be stopped in New Guinea and in the Solomons, so they ordered the construction of advanced staging bases in New Zealand, New Caledonia and the New Hebrides.

Political and labor difficulties and distances from the battlefields were to make the staging bases in New Zealand and New Caledonia of limited time value. On the other hand, the New Hebrides bases were destined to be major contributors to the conduct of the South Pacific campaign. The gamble was to pay off.

The New Hebrides of 1942 were an isolated chain of islands some 500 miles long populated by a stone-age people whose main source of income was from copra production. The rich volcanic soil and heavy rainfall produced lush,

The street between Areas 4 and 5 of the hospital compound at "Buttons." The Officer of the Day holds forth in the Quonset hut to the left. Servicemen are gathered at the Post Office hut on the right.

impenetrable tropical growth, one that harbored an abundance of malaria-carrying mosquitoes. These islands had one thing going for them, though. They were in the right place at the right time.

Efate, the capital island near the center of the chain, soon became an active staging base of its own with Havannah Harbor able to contain dozens of Navy combat and supply ships. But it was the large island of Espiritu Santo, 150 miles north of Efate, that was to be the big development.

Buttons Is Born

This staging base had a most colorful beginning, according to James Michener in his book *Tales of the South Pacific*: "I also knew Admiral (John) McCain in a very minor way. He was an ugly old aviator. One day he flew over Santo and pointed down at the island wilderness and said, 'That's where we'll

build our base.' And the base was built there, and millions of dollars were spent there, and everyone agrees that Santo was the best base the Navy ever built in the region."

The South Pacific war's major supply depot and staging base was to be hacked out of a jungle and made into an instant supermarket of war goods and services in an area most of the world had never heard of.

Five hundred U.S. Army National Guardsmen followed by the 4th Marine Defense Battalion and construction engineers immediately moved north from Efate on May 28, 1942, to establish the first airstrip on Espiritu Santo. It was still 550 miles from Guadalcanal, but within fighter delivery range and bomber radius of action.

The primitive airfield was constructed near the small village of Luganville on the banks of Segond Channel and it became known as "Bomber One." At that time, Luganville consisted of a Catholic mission, a few stores, the British and

Right: The waterfront and Segond Channel at Espiritu Santo, as it looked on Aug. 29, 1943. This was the Allies' primary supply and staging base for operations in the South Pacific.

Bottom: An aerial view of Luganville Field on Espiritu Santo in 1944. It became known as Bomber One.

Soldiers scramble down the side of the President Coolidge to be rescued after it hit a friendly mine at the entrance to Segond Channel. The ship soon after slid down into deeper water and sank on Oct. 25, 1942.

French district agencies and a hospital on the west side of the Sarakata River. It was soon to be eclipsed by the big staging base east of the river called "Buttons," but known to servicemen simply as "Santo" (short for Espiritu Santo), the name of the whole island.

Buttons became a city unto itself, serving a (very transient) population of 100,000 persons. As supply and headquarters base, it had the infrastructure of a small American city—excellent roads, telephone and teletype systems, PX, steam laundry, four well-equipped hospitals, an optical laboratory, endless warehouses and barracks.

For recreation there were movie houses, mess halls, ball fields, beer halls and what, at the time, was claimed to be the longest bar in the Pacific. Buttons was a boom town, but like all boom towns, it was destined to have a limited lifetime.

Three airfields handled aircraft ranging from B-17s to tiny reconnaissance planes and included a radio range for instrument approaches. Only one of the three original airfields remains in operation today, Bomber Two, and it is now called Pekoa Airport.

Navy PBYs operated from eastern harbors on Espiritu Santo, providing search and rescue service for the thousands of combat missions flown in the long battle for control of the Solomon Islands.

Air-sea rescue boats operated around the clock out of Palikulo Bay, now the site of the local yacht club and a Japanese fish-processing plant supplied with fish by Taiwanese fishing boats. Out in Segond Channel were moorings for dozens of combat, support and cargo ships.

There was little contact between natives and servicemen during Buttons' short life. The few-thousand natives living in the vicinity were moved out of the immediate area, although about 600 were employed as workers. French planters sent their daughters to another island where they would be safer.

Right: The ubiquitous Quonset huts were used for storage and shops for an aviation repair unit on Espiritu Santo.

Bottom: The original town of Luganville along the shoreline of the Segond Channel to the west of the Sarakata River in October 1942. Mission St. Michel is seen to the right. A U.S. Navy Consolidated PBY Catalina patrol bomber is moored in the channel.

Expatriate Tonkinese, in their wily manner, provided trade goods to the GIs and thus was born the "Bloody Mary" of Michener fame.

A Major Ship Casualty

Santo was far from the fighting front and, except for a few Japanese nuisance bombs dropped on it, all hazardous action was of the Allies' own doing.

The most notable of self-inflicted wounds was the loss of the USAT *President Coolidge*. The 22,000-ton *Coolidge* had been built in the 1930s for luxury travel to the Orient and was in her heyday at the start of the Pacific war. She was quickly converted to an Army troop transport and on Oct. 25, 1942, her seventh wartime mission, she headed into the harbor at Santo and became an innocent victim of "friendly fire." *Coolidge* had erred in her approach navigation and, despite frantic warnings signaled from shore, the vessel steamed into a minefield intended to thwart the entry of Japanese ships or submarines.

On encountering a mine, which blew a huge hole in the ship's hull, the captain wisely ran *Coolidge* aground and the 5,400 Army troops and ship's company clambered down cargo nets into the water for immediate rescue. The ship slipped backward into deeper water and sank 1 hour and 25 minutes after encountering the mines. Only nine men were lost in the sinking, but the fighting gear and supplies for a whole Army division were lost, as well as an irreplaceable supply of Atabrine destined for malaria-plagued troops on Guadalcanal. The luxury vessel turned warship is today a dramatic underwater museum.

Buttons Winds Down

When it became undeniably clear that the battlefront had permanently moved north of the equator and the vast quantity of supplies and equipment were no longer needed at this location, the question arose of what to do with it. There were not enough ships available to move it to the North Pacific, which was already being supplied by the largest and longest floating supply line ever assembled. American business didn't want it shipped back to the States and sold as surplus on the public market. Another idea was to offer it to the French and leave it on Santo for local use. The latter idea was the most practical so it was offered to the local French at a charge of 8 cents on the dollar. The French, however, held out for a "better deal."

It soon became urgent for the great South Pacific supply depot to close shop and move on north to the new fighting front. With no counteroffer in hand from the French, GIs simply bulldozed millions of dollars of food, tools, repair parts

and clothing into a coral borrow pit fronting Segond Channel.

Bulldozers, jeeps, forklifts and any vehicle that could move under its own power were simply driven into the ocean. This went on for days until the great base at Santo was denuded of supplies. It was then closed and the personnel transferred to the war effort up north.

This great dump is no longer visible to the naked eye, but the fish in Segond Channel gained a new and expensive habitat. The location is, appropriately, named "Million Dollar Point" and is a scuba diver's paradise.

New Hebrides Today

The postwar period did not automatically bring an end to the New Hebrides' awkward condominium government. The condominium had been established in 1914 after ceaseless talks by the French and British failed to yield an agreement on who should govern this colonial island group.

To the detriment of the people, it was finally declared a region of joint interest to be administered by a condominium government. Joint colonial administrations were set up giving the New Hebrides two sets of colonial laws, plus native laws, and separate British and French police forces, hospitals and government offices. Each used its own national language and its own system of weights, measures and currency. Pandemonium reigned for years in the condominium colony.

In 1980, the British and French were finally able to agree on one thing—independence for the people of the New Hebrides. A government was elected for the new country, to be called Vanuatu. For the first time in 154 years, the ni-Vanuatu (as the people of Vanuatu are known) were free of foreign domination.

Most of modern Luganville now lies on the eastern side of the Sarakata River where Buttons was built. Quonset huts are still very much in evidence, serving as warehouses, shops and homes. Marston airstrip matting still serves as building material and fencing. Main Street is one mile long, running on the terrace above the wharves. It is the widest street in the South Pacific and undeniably the dustiest.

Luganville had its most prosperous period just after World War II when a boom in copra coincided with the acquisition of a ready-made town formerly called Buttons. Prosperity did not last for many years, however. The price of copra dropped, 2,000 energetic Vietnamese were repatriated to their homeland and the economy turned, once again, to subsistence agriculture.

Prosperity has proven a will-o'-the-wisp for the ni-Vanuatu, but they still have something the Western world dreams of—the island of Aoba, 40 miles to the east of Espiritu Santo, better known to James Michener's fans as Bali Hai.

CHAPTER 1

PEARL HARBOR

Top: Waikiki Beach today. The venerable Royal Hawaiian Hotel stands dwarfed by the Sheraton Waikiki Hotel. The beach teems with overseas visitors, many from Japan, which decades ago had other designs on Hawaii.

Middle: The Pearl Harbor Naval Shipyard today. Inexplicably, the shipyard largely escaped the attention of the attackers, which accounted for its ability to begin immediate repairs on the ships that were damaged in the raid.

Bottom: The World War II Arizona memorial sits athwart the sunken battleship in Pearl Harbor. The remains of more than 1,100 sailors remain in the hulk, which today is still considered a commissioned ship.

CHAPTER 2

WAKE ISLAND

Right: All that remains of Pan American's pre-World War II seaplane pier on Peale Island. Pan American Airways has also ceased to exist in today's highly competitive air transportation world.

Left: Transportation to Wake Island is provided by USAF Lockheed C-141 transport planes.

Bottom Left: In 1942 the Japanese evacuated all U.S. servicemen and all but 98 civilian workers from Wake Island. In 1943, those 98 POWs were executed, ostensibly for making contact with American forces. More likely, it was because of a food shortage brought on by a tight naval blockade. This rock, near the execution site, became their memorial.

Bottom Right: This memorial to the courageous Marine defenders of Wake Island stands near their World War II command post.

CHAPTER 3

MIDWAY

Left: Former cable station employee quarters built on Sand Island in 1905 are now on the National Register of Historic Places. (Photo courtesy of PHC Larry Krause, USNR)

Right: Life on Midway comes complete with a mall and the ever-present gooney birds (Laysan albatross), which are a protected species.

Below: Midway Islands circa 1990. Eastern Island in the background was developed prior to World War II, and Sand Island in the foreground was developed during and after the war. Eastern Island has been abandoned to wildlife. The submarine refueling harbor on Sand Island is clearly visible at left center of photo. (US Navy photo)

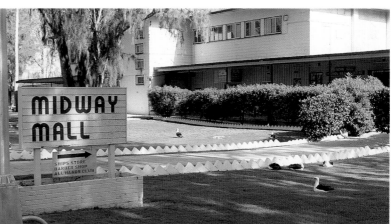

CHAPTER 4

GUADALCANAL

*Right: Solomon Islanders
are a handsome and
dignified people living
in a period that embraces
both a subsistence and
cash economy.*

*Below: The international
airport terminal on the site
of Henderson Field near
Honiara.*

Red Beach today displays only a small amount of litter from the American landings.

Children play near the mouth of the Matanikau River where so much heavy fighting took place during the dark days of the Guadalcanal campaign.

CHAPTER 5

TARAWA

Right: The author's wife is entertained by local children on Red Beach 2 where a relic of war is part of their playground.

Below: The lagoon is quiet now. A Gilbertese takes his sailing pleasure inside Tarawa Atoll's lagoon where decades ago death was the order of the day.

Above: Flourishing coconut palms and green grass have transformed the Japanese bombproof command post into an almost park-like scene. Such installations covered with coconut logs and sand were virtually impervious to shellfire, even from battleships' 16-inch guns, and had to be taken by direct assault. The Betio fortifications were considered the best engineered of all defenses in Japan's Pacific islands.

Left: Annually, Japanese visit their battleground shrines and pay homage to their lost soldiers. The event on Betio draws the attention of the local people.

CHAPTER 6

MARSHALL ISLANDS

Left: Kwajalein Island is now the home of the U.S. Army Kwajalein Atoll Command. Nearly 3,000 persons live and work on this island as part of the strategic defense research and technology validation programs. Roi and Namur are about 40 miles to the north.

Left: Copra, crafts, a developing fisheries industry and Kwajalein Atoll support are the mainstays of the Marshalls economy. This craftswoman works in the shade of a pandanus tree under the supervision of her children.

Below: Ruins of the Japanese communications station on Jaluit Atoll, which was taken by American troops with little resistance. Jaluit was the administrative headquarters of the Japanese and, earlier, the Germans.

CHAPTER 7

RABAUL

Right: Boys pose at the mouth of a barge tunnel at Karavia Bay, outside Rabaul. Five barges were lined up on a minirailroad so they could be launched into the bay to receive cargo from Japanese submarines. They were then pulled back onto the rails and into the cave for unloading while hidden from allied planes.

Bottom: The main street of Rabaul before the 1994 volcanic eruptions. The entire city was blanketed by layers of ash and other debris.

Among the fruits of victory for the Japanese in the conquest of Singapore was this heavy-lift barge crane brought to Rabaul to service their naval vessels. Allied planes sunk it at its mooring.

Burns-Philp, an early South Seas trader, stills gathers and markets the products of the islands. Converted landing ships are ideal for serving outer islands not having docking facilities.

CHAPTER 8

PAPUA NEW GUINEA
(New Guinea)

Right: The people of Hanuabada village were land-dwellers at one time, but tribal warfare drove them off the land onto the stilt houses now seen in Moresby Harbor. The city of Port Moresby is seen in the background.

Left: A workhorse of World War II, a DC-3 Dakota transport, is a fitting memorial at the entrance to Port Moresby's Jackson International Airport, itself a memento of World War II.

Bottom Left: The coastwatchers, mostly Australians and New Zealanders who lived and worked in the New Guinea and Solomon Islands before hostilities, provided timely information on Japanese movements and helped save downed Allied airmen. This memorial to their bravery is at Madang.

Bottom Right: The National Parliament of Papua New Guinea meets in this neoclassic building in a suburb of Port Moresby, there to administer the affairs of state of a wide-flung 626-island country.

CHAPTER 9

VANUATU
(New Hebrides)

Left: Laundry day at Eton Beach, Efate Island—not much different than when Allied troops and ships were present during World War II.

Middle: The new Luganville waterfront intermingled with the old.

Bottom Left: The main street of modern Luganville parallels the waterfront as it did when Buttons occupied the site. This is probably the widest and dustiest street in the South Pacific.

Bottom Right: A scuba diver emerges from the water at the site of the sinking of the transport President Coolidge. This site and that of Million Dollar Point, just to the left of the photo, are favorite dive sites for scuba enthusiasts from around the world.

CHAPTER 10

CHUUK
(Truk)

Right: An unsophisticated gasoline service station on Moen serves the needs of island automobiles.

Below: The local population make the most of old Japanese facilities. A corner of the seaplane ramp at Dublon with its natural drainage has become the laundry room for this woman.

The heavily armored communications station on Dublon Island was no match for the bombs of Allied planes.

One of the most famous schools of the Pacific is Xavier High School on Moen Island (now called Weno Island). It is housed in a former communications building made of one-meter-thick reinforced concrete that was oblivious to bombing. The school is operated by the Jesuit Order, which chose to retain the building's World War II appearance.

CHAPTER 11

SAIPAN

Right: World War II Japanese artillery and other weapons lie outside the Japanese "Last Command Post," a cleverly disguised natural cave used also as a lookout point against the American forces advancing across the Tanapeg plain.

Middle Left: "Banzai Cliff" at Marpi Point, where thousands of Japanese troops and civilians jumped to their deaths rather than be captured by American forces. It is now a memorial that is visited regularly by tourists.

Middle Right: Few relics of World War II remain on the island. This Japanese tank is one of them resting atop a fortified position in the shade of a flame tree. The location is along Beach Road midway between Garapan and Charan Kanoa.

Left: A World War II Japanese blockhouse near Aslito Airfield (now Iseley International Airport). Today it serves as a personnel shelter for Saipan's continuing other enemy, the typhoon.

CHAPTER 12

GUAM

Left: The recreational boating facility at Agana Bay adjacent to the American landing sites at Asan Bay. The Japanese kept the Marines at the Asan Bay beachhead pinned down for five days before they could break through the heavy defenses.

Middle Left: Relics of World War II are sparse on Guam. This Japanese tank found an unusual use in an American political campaign.

Middle Right: Tourists visit the postwar Magellan monument at Umatec Bay. This bay was the landing point for Spanish galleons sailing from Manila to Acapulco in the 18th century. Ironically, most of Guam's tourists today are from Japan.

Right: Latte Stone Park in Agana did not exist at the time of the invasion. It was created in postwar years to illustrate the use of the unusual markers believed to support the houses of the "ancients." The stones are found throughout the Mariana Islands and are treated with almost religious respect.

CHAPTER 13

PELELIU

Right: The waters around Peleliu, once the scene of warships and landing craft, now are a favorite of scuba divers from around the world. Photo courtesy of Judy/Corydon Wagner, Jr.

Below: Palauan children play around a Japanese antiaircraft gun, a relic of World War II. Photo courtesy of Judy/Corydon Wagner, Jr.

Bottom Left: The 1,000-man "navy cave" on Peleliu is an example of how well-entrenched the Japanese defenders were. Photo courtesy of Karl Bielan.

Bottom Right: American veterans of the battle of Peleliu returned years later to pay homage to their fallen comrades at the 1st Marine Division memorial on Bloody Nose Ridge. Photo courtesy of Judy Wagner.

TRUK
"Gibraltar of the Pacific" Neutralized

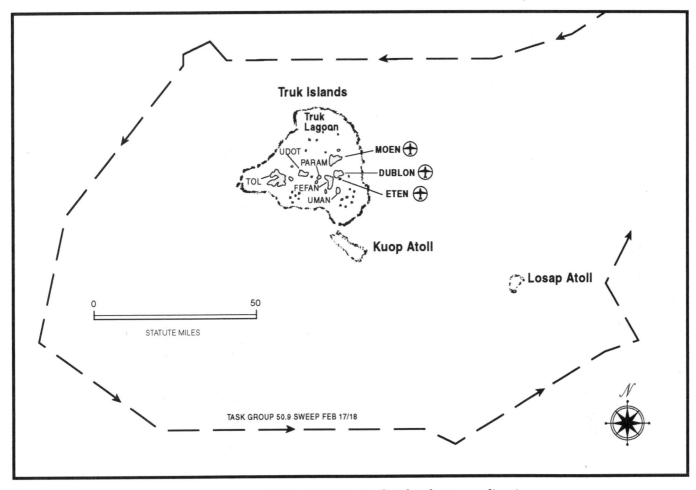

Truk Islands

Truk Lagoon

UDOT

PARAM

TOL

FEFAN

UMAN

MOEN ⊕

DUBLON ⊕

ETEN ⊕

Kuop Atoll

Losap Atoll

0   50

STATUTE MILES

TASK GROUP 50.9 SWEEP FEB 17/18

N

U.S. Operation HAILSTONE -Truk Islands Neutralization

At one time, millions of years ago, Truk was one big island, a rolling mountainous hulk with today's Udot Island at its approximate center. Slowly the island sank. Finally, only the highest peaks of the prehistoric mountains remained above water.

In the meantime, energetic coral polyps built their fringing reef around the sinking island, creating the mighty Truk lagoon. People arrived from somewhere in southeast Asia. Life flourished and those first settlers were satisfied to till the soil, fish the lagoon and climb the coconut palms.

It was the Spanish merchant fleet that first brought the affairs of the Western world to Micronesia. They sold out to the Germans after the Spanish-American War. Then came World War I, and Japan occupied all of Micronesia except Guam, an American territory.

After World War I, the League of Nations formally, if somewhat reluctantly, mandated Micronesia to Japan. But then, in 1935, Japan withdrew from the League and made the islands part of their Greater East Asia Co-Prosperity Sphere. The door to Micronesia was closed to the rest of the world. The handwriting was on the wall for all to see, but who could read it?

Behind those closed doors Japan plotted the further expansion of its empire that was to embroil the peoples of the Pacific in four years of hell. Certain islands of Micronesia were tagged to play significant roles in Japan's future. Truk was one. With a sheltered lagoon more than 800 square miles in area and several substantial islands for land bases within it, Truk was to become a major offensive naval base.

Work on naval and air shore facilities was secretly start-

Cruiser Duluth *of Task Force 38 rides peacefully at anchor in Truk Lagoon after the cessation of hostilities with the Japanese.*

ed on several islands of Truk and in 1939 it became the headquarters of the Japanese 4th Fleet. One year later, Japan started adding defensive capabilities to Truk while its Pacific neighbors slept.

The alarm went off on Dec. 7, 1941, when the Japanese attacked Pearl Harbor. The attack was successful beyond Japan's wildest dreams, but the Japanese military had awakened a sleeping giant. It was to eventually destroy their dream of the Greater East Asia Co-Prosperity Sphere and all but destroy the empire itself.

An aura of mystery had always surrounded Truk. Japan allowed no news to get out regarding its Micronesian holdings. Intelligence efforts were foiled by an alert Japan. Not until January 1942 were aerial photographs of Truk taken by an Australian Air Force plane. They showed large land installations and many ships present in the harbor, giving rise to the myth of the "Gibraltar of the Pacific." And truly a myth it was, for as the Japanese commander of Truk, Admiral Hara,

remarked after the war: "I feared, lest the Americans find out how weak it was."

Inside Truk Atoll

Of the 11 islands inside Truk lagoon, Japan had chosen Dublon (called "Summer" by the Japanese) as its headquarters and built an extensive submarine and seaplane base on it. Neighboring Moen ("Spring"), the second largest in the group, was made the location of heavy coast and antiaircraft artillery plus two major airfields. It looked out over the north and northeast passes. Little Eten ("Bamboo"), only 86 acres, had its topography rearranged to resemble an aircraft carrier. Other islands had lesser military assignments, but had major roles as suppliers of food for the military forces.

Trukese were moved from Dublon, Moen and Eten to the outer islands as agrarian workers. After Japan occupied Nauru Island to the south, in 1945, 1,200 Nauruans (two-

Right: A Japanese munitions ship blows up in Truk lagoon during an attack by carrier planes.

Bottom: Douglas SBD Dauntless dive-bombers (close up and bottom right) and Grumman TBF Avenger torpedo bombers (top right), launched from American carriers of Task Force 58, fly over Truk Lagoon on their way to raid Dublon (upper left) and Moen (out of picture at left). Other islands in photo include Fefan, Eten, Uman, Rsis, Tarik and part of Param.

Dublon town burns furiously after the April 30, 1944, raid by carrier planes.

thirds of Nauru's entire population) were transported to Truk to increase the agricultural labor force. Living and working conditions were so poor that more than one-third of the Nauruans died on Truk.

Truk's defenses were well planned, with coast artillery commanding the five entrances to the lagoon, while smaller artillery on the barrier reef islands would prevent landings there. The five entrances to the lagoon all were mined, as were the inner channels. Army troops and Naval Guard units numbering in excess of 24,000 men were garrisoned at Truk. An estimated 365 aircraft were in place, although they came and went as resupply of Rabaul took place. Truk's defenses were significant enough to deter a landing force, but its real defense was to be the Imperial Fleet, which at midpoint in the war was being severely tested in other parts of the Pacific and never showed up for the neutralization party.

In 1942 and 1943, America and its Allies were busy containing the Pacific invader in the southern hemisphere, but they couldn't help noting that Truk was the keystone of Japanese South Pacific supply routes. Through it flowed many of the men and much of the materiel that menaced General MacArthur in New Guinea and Admiral Nimitz in the Solomons. They knew that Rabaul's supply line came through Truk, and planes from Truk harassed Allied forces on all fronts. Truk had to be put out of the way, but how?

If, indeed, Truk was a "Gibraltar," invasion was out of the question. The lessons of Tarawa were still too fresh. The strategy leaned heavily toward neutralization, the process that eventually put Rabaul out of the war. Allied intelligence was supported by photographs taken on Feb. 5, 1944, by long-range Marine B-24 Liberators.

The results of that flight were mixed—American forces got valuable intelligence, but the planes alerted the Japanese to Truk's vulnerability and most of the 5th Japanese Fleet, including the superbattleship *Musashi*, was sortied immediately to the relative safety of Palau.

Bomb craters and wrecked planes litter the Japanese seaplane base on Moen Island after an American air raid.

Operation Hailstone Begins

The neutralization of Truk by Operation Hailstone started on February 17 and 18, with heavy attacks by aircraft from five American carriers from Task Force 58 under Adm. Marc Mitscher. As a measure of the intensity of the two-day attack, each of the 30 air strikes flown against Truk was more intense than either of the two Japanese strikes made against Pearl Harbor.

While airplanes attacked the island, a surface battlefleet under Adm. Raymond Spruance cruised around the atoll to challenge any ships that might escape from the lagoon. His screening force destroyed one cruiser.

In all, the Japanese lost more than 250 airplanes, 137,000 tons of ships and an unknown number of personnel. The American forces had only one ship damaged, 25 airplanes lost and 40 personnel killed. Much of the credit for the small loss in downed air crews goes to the gutsy rescue work of submarines and seaplanes.

The enemy's ability to carry on in spite of heavy losses was well known from experience in other Pacific theaters, so it was deemed necessary to continue the neutralization process. In a second major carrier raid made on April 30 and May 1, many of the remaining Japanese aircraft were destroyed as well as all new resupply ships found in the lagoon.

For the rest of the war, Truk became an Army Air Force show. Proven B-24s and the new B-29s flying from recently acquired bases continued a heavy bombardment of the atoll.

But a persistent heavy defense on the ground and in the air proved that the Truk defenders were well dug in and could patch airplanes together literally overnight.

Truk took on a most unusual role as the war progressed. It became a training target for air crews. This was especially true after Britain shifted major elements of its Navy to the Pacific following the collapse of Germany in May 1945. Not even the "Gibraltar of the Pacific" could stand up to such continued destruction, and Japanese defenses wasted away awaiting the end of the war.

Fighting on Truk ceased on Aug. 15, 1945 (Japan date), with the capitulation of all Japanese forces. Formal surrender of the Truk garrison took place on September 2, aboard the USS *Portland* in Truk Harbor, simultaneously with that in Tokyo Bay. The "Gibraltar of the Pacific" was no more—if it ever had been.

Chuuk State Emerges

The Truk Islands, along with the rest of Japan's Micronesia, became the Trust Territory of the Pacific Islands after the war, to be administered by the United States under United Nations mandate. In contrast to the religious goals of the Spanish, the trading goals of the Germans and the militaristic goals of the Japanese, the Americans allowed the economy and society of Micronesia to drift along seeking its own future. It rapidly became known as the "Rust Territory," with benign neglect being the order of the day.

Not until the late 1970s was enough pressure exerted on

the United States by the Micronesians and some UN observers to cause the United States to develop island infrastructures and begin talks on Micronesian independence. In 1978, the people of Truk, along with those of Kosrae, Pohnpei and Yap, united as the Federated States of Micronesia (FSM) in free association with the United States. The trust agreement was finally terminated in 1990.

The idea of a free and independent Federated States of Micronesia with a government founded on the democratic principles of the United States is a noble goal, but can island peoples with few resources stand alone as democracy suggests?

Democracy requires the creation of wealth to support it, something the FSM is not likely to be able to do. That leaves the United States with the responsibility to subsidize not only the FSM, but the other emerging nations of the former trust territory. This will be a drain on United States resources not anticipated when it accepted, or more correctly, requested accountability for the islands of Micronesia to prevent their use by any other foreign power.

Today's Truk has a different name; it is now Chuuk and the people are "Chuukese." It is still an agrarian society with strong overtones of Western civilization wreaking havoc with its people. Beer, cars, tobacco and boom boxes use up much of the people's resources.

Underemployed men have tended to violence in both the home and on the streets, keeping all but the most determined of tourists away. These tourists are the scuba divers who come to see the "Ghost Fleet of the Truk Lagoon"—a collection of 60 Japanese vessels sunk during the war and constituting one of the most exciting underwater museums in the world.

The lagoon is peaceful now. Trade winds caress the palms and fish leap out of water at dusk. Man-made beasts of war have been replaced by nature's wondrous rags. The Chuukese, now more or less on their own, are seeking to renew pride in their heritage. They know success will come their way, for they have an expression: "What the tide washes ashore, it will one day take away."

CHAPTER 11

SAIPAN
A Battle for the High Ground

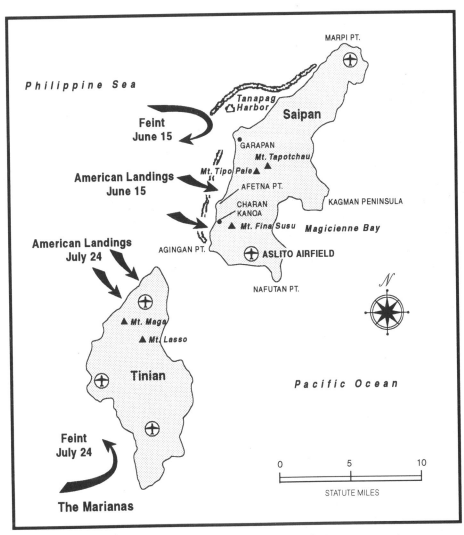

U.S. Operation FORAGER - Saipan and Tinian Invasions

Thwarted by failure of their Greater East Asia Co-Prosperity Sphere to expand in the South Pacific, Japanese Imperialists began to think in terms of establishing defensive lines to protect what they already had conquered. They were also becoming concerned about the vulnerability of their home islands to enemy attack as the American forces grew stronger.

They looked toward the Marshall Islands as an outer line of defense, with the Caroline and Mariana Islands as the inner lines. Except for Guam, the Japanese had "owned and occupied" all of these central Pacific islands since World War I and were still overly confident that these islands could form an effective invasion barrier. Ironically, they still didn't believe in the mobility of aircraft carriers as an offensive force, a weapon they themselves had employed so successfully at Pearl Harbor.

Throughout most of the earlier South Pacific campaigns, the Americans had the benefit of British, Dutch and Australian intelligence to aid in battle planning. But the Japanese had effectively denied intelligence gathering in the mandated islands, so stories grew of the invincibility of these islands whose defenses had supposedly been built over a long period of time.

It was suspected that thousands of Japanese soldiers occupying these islands had strongly fortified them in anticipation of coming American attacks. Parts of the stories were true, parts were illusionary, fostered by early Japanese suc-

Left: Army reinforcements arriving by LST had a long, exposed march across the coral reef to the beach.

Bottom: The tension of battle clearly shows on the face of this Marine during an advance across Saipan.

Bottom Right: A Marine keeps watch from his post in a captured Japanese blockhouse, carved into the limestone of a Saipan hill.

cesses and the American experience at the unusually well fortified island of Betio in Tarawa.

After Guadalcanal was secured, American forces, bolstered in numbers, equipment and confidence, changed their strategy to concentrate naval, ground and air forces in overwhelming numbers on just a few targets, thereby assuring success with minimum losses. Some strong-point islands could be neutralized by naval gunfire and aerial bombings. Other islands could be simply bypassed and left to wither on the vine. The list of required invasion targets was narrowed to just a few that would provide the best bases as steppingstones to Tokyo.

American forces then began whittling away at Japan's outer line of defense in the islands of Micronesia. First came Tarawa and Makin in the Gilberts, then Kwajalein and Eniwetok in the Marshalls. Along with the occupation of these islands, American forces neutralized others. The loss of men and materiel on all of these islands, especially the important staging site at Truk, was a major blow to the Japanese. The most disconcerting fact, though, was that the Americans were moving westward at a swift pace and an attack on the Marianas was not far off.

Target: Marianas

To Japan, the islands of Rota, Tinian and Saipan had become like its home islands. By 1938, some 45,000 Japanese had moved to Saipan to live and work. Japanese immigrants represented 90 percent of the island's population, having, in effect, pushed the native Chamorros off the island. (In 1942 Japanese immigrants in all of the mandated islands numbered 96,000, almost 50 percent of the population.)

Sugar and its vital byproducts were produced in the Marianas for consumption by the home islands. The Marianas could not now be abandoned nor could its people continue their peaceful agrarian life.

Japan's commander in the Marianas, General Saito, ordered his forces to make Saipan into an "invulnerable

Bombed and shelled to smithereens, war-ravaged Garapan gives mute testimony to the ferocity of the fighting on Saipan. Tourism is helping the town return to its former status as the island's administrative center.

After the Marines captured this mountain gun from the Japanese at Saipan, they returned it to good use during the attack on Garapan.

fortress," which was not to be an easy nor leisurely task. Japanese military planners had not reckoned with the rapid advance of American forces through the central Pacific and so were unprepared.

Furthermore, Japan no longer controlled the sea lanes between Japan and the Marianas. They found this out the hard way when they attempted to evacuate civilians from the islands. Convoys carrying evacuees from the Marianas and military supplies to the Marianas were attacked and decimated by American submarines and far-ranging carrier aircraft. Nevertheless, defense preparations continued with the supplies on hand and the 30,000 troops already on Saipan.

The Japanese army proceeded as best and as fast as it could with the fortification of Saipan. The island covered 46

Marines and amphtracs begin piling up on the beach as the initial assault waves invade Saipan on June 15, 1944.

square miles of irregular terrain. The eastern side had high cliffs above its coral reefs. The western side had low coastal lands whose reefs were broken in a few places, making them suitable for seaborne landings.

But Japanese defense planners were hung up on meeting the enemy on the beaches and denying him entry to the island. This doctrine was apropos to atolls, whose highest ground was a mere 10 to 12 feet above sea level, yielding no topographic advantage to either side, but it failed to take advantage of the naturally high ground of Saipan's interior, which rose to 1,600 feet. As a result, Saipan's defenses were fatally compromised by the military's fixation with atoll defense.

Japan had yet another worry in preparing its defense of the Mariana Islands. Her naval and air fleets had been badly battered in the South Pacific. The once mighty Combined Fleet had too few ships, too few planes and too few experienced pilots. Further, its reserves of petroleum were in short supply, requiring that most of the fleet be kept close to fuel supplies in the Dutch East Indies or the Philippines. The Combined Fleet was impotent to do anything but wait for a chance opportunity to make a final and conclusive attack on the far-ranging armada of American ships operating ever closer to the Japanese home islands.

America, too, had to think seriously about its attack on Saipan, which was expected to be the most heavily defended of the Marianas. Larger Guam, 120 miles to the south, was not so heavily defended because it had been an unfortified

American territory prior to World War II. It was also farther away from Japan. The belief was held that the Japanese considered Guam to be expendable in the long run, but that they still intended to put up a good battle as the later invasion of Guam would prove. The choice to the American high command was clear. It had to be Saipan, a formidable undertaking.

D-day for Saipan

Preliminary naval bombardment of the island began in earnest on June 13, 1944, two days prior to D-day. On D-day, a Marine landing feint was made in the vicinity of Tanapag Harbor. It did nothing but give Radio Tokyo a new story about how the Americans tried to land and were driven off. Actually, not a shot was fired and the feint failed.

The real invasion by elements of the 2nd and 4th Marine Divisions under Gen. "Howling Mad" Smith took place to the south along the beaches of Afetna Point and Charon Kanoa. Wave after wave of landing craft and amphtracs came ashore. Marines soon established a line a few hundred yards inland and dug in against a withering enemy return fire and Japanese counterattacks. More Marines came ashore along with elements of the Army 27th Infantry Division under Gen. Ralph Smith, and the drive continued to Aslito airfield (now Saipan's Isely International Airport) and then turned north up the island.

Army infantrymen close in on a Japanese sniper's fox-hole during mop-up-operations on Saipan.

The invasion might not have gone so well had the Japanese fleet leaving the Philippines for the Marianas not been intercepted by the Navy's famous Task Force 58. For several days the two fleets spied on each other by plane and submarine. Then on June 19 they locked horns in a day-long aerial battle that ranged between 30 and 150 miles northwest of Guam. The Japanese lost 476 airplanes while the Americans lost 130. The battle, officially known as the Battle of the Philippine Sea, has gone down in history as "The Great Marianas Turkey Shoot" and the end of Japanese naval air power in the Pacific.

Back on Saipan, one week after the initial landings, the battle lines had advanced almost halfway up the 14-mile-long island into mountainous terrain. The major town of Garapan had been taken on June 24. Finally, the remaining Japanese forces and many civilians were driven north to Marpi Point, where they chose to commit suicide by leaping off the 800-foot precipice rather than surrender.

By July 9, U.S. forces had swept the full length and breadth of the island, and the American flag was officially raised over Saipan on July 10. Newly garrisoned American troops, however, would be kept busy for at least another three weeks rooting out knots of Japanese soldiers hiding in caves.

The human losses on Saipan were great—Japanese dead estimated at 24,000 (23,811 were buried by actual count), 1,780 prisoners of war taken and 14,560 civilians interned. The Americans counted 3,426 dead plus another 13,099 wounded. Ironically, the United States had rejected Saipan as a spoil of war at the end of the Spanish-American War in 1898. Now it came back as an expensive responsibility.

Saipan was devastated by the fighting and made completely devoid of buildings and trees, but the Americans wasted no time restoring it as a base for launching bombing raids on Japan. With the fall of Saipan, both Tinian and Rota were captured with relative ease. Tinian went on to become the base from which the B-29s took off for the atomic bombing of Hiroshima and Nagasaki, putting an end to the war.

Saipan Chooses U.S. Commonwealth Status

Saipan has recovered from its World War II destruction and, after years as part of the Trust Territory of the Pacific Islands, the people of the Northern Marianas elected to become a self-governing commonwealth of the United States. There is no question that they are succeeding. Their source of wealth, though, is none other than their former occupation masters—the Japanese.

Tourists numbering about 500,000 a year come mostly from Japan. The numbers are not surprising since Japan is only 1,200 miles away and to the Japanese the warm climate, open space and low prices of Saipan are a tonic to harassed living in crowded Tokyo. Their upscale spending has created new hotels, restaurants and night clubs on Saipan.

Today, Saipan's economic situation is one to envy. There is the ever-increasing flow of tourists, heavy investment of foreign (spelled J-a-p-a-n-e-s-e) money with virtually no investment control, few government regulations on zoning or building, and a low minimum wage. More than half of the population is now made up of alien workers from the Philippines, China and other Asian countries. It is an attractive situation in the short run, but poses long-term political problems as it has in Fiji. Warned by the United States about the consequences of such a trend, the Saipanese reply it is their choice. The youthful country still has much to learn, as more recent alien-labor problems have surfaced, bringing much criticism from the United States and other nations.

CHAPTER 12

GUAM
The Taking and the Retaking

U.S. Operation FORAGER - Guam Recaptured

World War II started for Guam on Dec. 8, 1941 (Guamanian time), with an air raid on military targets in the Sumay-Piti-Apra Harbor area by nine Saipan-based Japanese bombers. It came as no surprise to the governor, U. S. Navy Capt. George McMillin, who had already received word by radio of the Pearl Harbor attack, but there was little he could do about it. Congress had decided in 1938 that establishing military defenses on Guam would provoke the Japanese into attacking, so nothing was done. But they still attacked.

Guam's meager military defenses consisted of the Insular Guard Force, three small naval vessels, and the Marine Barracks. Weaponry was mostly .30-cal. rifles and .45-cal. pistols, with one machine gun nest at lower Tamuning.

The first 400 Japanese invasion troops, under the overall command of General Goto, landed within 48 hours near Agana and overran the Insular Guard Force. Simultaneously, the main Japanese Army invasion force of 5,500 troops landed below Agat. It took only a few hours after their arrival to convince McMillin that any defense of the island was futile. He signed papers of surrender at 6 a.m. December 10. For the next 2-1/2 years, Guamanians lived and died under a harsh Japanese occupation.

For the first three months the Japanese Invasion Army ruled Guam with an iron fist to break the spirit of the Guamanians. Executions became the order of the day and any offense, from aiding American prisoners of war (before they were shipped off to Japan) to stealing food, was punishable by death.

Not since the days of the Spanish-Chamorro wars of the late 17th century had the people of Guam been subjected to

American troops use hand grenades and rifles to clean out a cave sheltering Japanese snipers. The hilly terrain and jungle made pursuit of the enemy slow work.

"Corporal Kurt," a Marine Corps war dog who was wounded with his Leatherneck partner, is given first aid in the field.

such repression. It was a welcome day in March 1942 when the Japanese Army units were shipped off to Rabaul to suffer their own endless hell on New Britain.

Japanese Navy rule followed and it was less repressive. The Japanese did, however, have the task of routing out the half-dozen Americans known to have escaped from Japanese captivity. Any Guamanians suspected of helping the escapees were physically punished. Eventually, only one American was on the loose and he, Navy radioman George Tweed, survived the war hiding on the island.

(A Japanese soldier, Shoichi Tokoi, later survived capture by the Americans in 1944. Hunters discovered him living in a cave in the jungle in 1972 and he was eventually repatriated to Japan.)

The American invasion fleet stands offshore at Asan in July 1944. Japanese resistance from this high ground inflicted heavy casualties on the U.S. troops initially.

The Japanese aimed to make Guam a part of its Greater East Asia Co-Prosperity Sphere. They named the island Omiya Jima, meaning Great Shrine Island. Japanese language schools appeared and Japanese became the lingua franca of the island. Punishment, torture and beheadings were generously used to influence Guamanians, but it didn't work. Guamanians remembered a better life and were not swayed in their hearts.

Hundreds of Guamanians fled to caves and the bush in the northern part of the island to avoid serving the Japanese and undergoing the Japanification process. Their little world became one of avoiding capture, finding food and worrying about their kin.

Troops from Manchuria

As American military forces continued to whittle away at the Japanese empire elsewhere, thousands of Japanese troops from Manchuria were sent to Guam, as were agricultural shock troops intended to increase the food productivity of the island. Every Guamanian except the ill, very young and aged were put to work in the fields. But the Guamanians sensed that the Americans could not be far away and they lived in hope. Then on Feb. 23, 1944, American carrier aircraft bombed the Orote airstrip, an answer to Guamanian prayers.

American plans to invade Guam were timed to take place a few days after the initial Saipan invasion. They were thwarted, however, by the Battle of the Philippine Sea and the unexpectedly heavy resistance put up by the Japanese on Saipan. Additional troops were needed for the invasion, and those troops were the 77th Infantry Division in Hawaii. As a result, the invasion date, "W-day" (Guam's D-day), was reset to July 21 to give time to transport the troops to the western Pacific.

Softening Up Continues

The time delay was used differently by each side. American forces continued their sea and air bombardment of Guam, and the Marine invasion forces rested at Eniwetok awaiting the arrival of the 77th Division.

The Japanese, under General Takashima, used the time to shore up their defenses, using the backbreaking labor of Guamanians and imported Korean slaves. Orote airstrip was repaired and new ones built at Tiyan and Dededo in hopes that Japan's once formidable air force would appear. It didn't, for it no longer existed.

Roads, air-raid shelters, pillboxes and gun emplacements were built on the western beaches. Underwater obstacles were built to slow the landing of invasion forces. Lacking cement and other materials for tetrahedron tank traps, they

Amphibious "Ducks" churn toward the beach landing areas loaded with Marines.

built cribs of coral. These, however, were easily destroyed by American underwater demolition teams in nightly forays along the beaches prior to the American invasion.

As American air raids intensified, Guamanians were moved to concentration camps in the northern part of the island. The island defenders with their backs to the wall knew they faced a fight for survival.

The real preinvasion bombardment by surface ships started on July 19, concentrating on two beaches—Asan to the north of Orote Peninsula and Agat to the south. The defenders realized these were the key landing points (they had also used them) and moved their mobile forces to the surrounding hills.

At 0600 on July 21, the invasion began. Asan was invaded by the 3rd Marine Division under Gen. Allen Turnage, while Agat was invaded by the 1st Provisional Marine Brigade under Gen. Lemuel Shepherd. The 77th Division under Gen. Andrew Bruce became the second wave of the Agat invasion.

With the Japanese dug in on the high ground overlooking both beaches, the invaders suffered initial heavy losses. It took several days for the troops to dig out the defenders in the surrounding hills. On July 28 the 1st Marine Brigade managed to take control of the Orote peninsula and the prewar Marine Barracks, a proud moment for them.

For a brief period, the war was locally halted while the Marines again raised the American flag at the barracks site. "To the Colors" was played on a captured Japanese bugle. Naval gunfire and aerial bombardment had carefully minimized damage to the airstrip at Orote so that within two days the engineers had it operational again.

Island Cut in Half

Meanwhile the 77th Division pushed east and north from Agat and joined up with the 3rd Marine Division coming off the Asan beaches. That pincer essentially cut the island in

Right: Marines take cover among fallen coconut palms and jungle brush while flushing out Japanese snipers during the fighting on Guam in July 1944.

Bottom: The first flag back on Guam flies from a makeshift boathook mast. Two U.S. officers planted the American flag just eight minutes after Marines and Army assault troops landed on the island.

half, but few Japanese defenders were left in the southern half as Japanese defense strategy called for a final stand to the northeast. The Marines and Army in eight days of fighting had secured half of the island and decimated about half of the defender's 19,000 troops.

From July 29 to August 10, the Marines and infantry advanced hesitatingly northward toward Mt. Santa Rosa, where Japanese General Obata had chosen to make his last stand. Along the way Chamorros took every opportunity to escape from their captors and flee behind the American lines. The 77th got the assignment to take Mt. Santa Rosa, which it did on August 8 with relatively light casualties. The 77th and the 3rd Marines spent the final days mopping up the enemy, who melted away into the forest to the north.

Guam was fully reclaimed by August 10. Of the 55,000 American forces deployed in this action, 1,435 were killed or missing in action, with another 5,650 wounded. Of the 19,000 Japanese on the island, most were believed to have been killed, since few prisoners surrendered.

Freedom Has Its Problems

Guam, 50 years later, is faced with an ironic set of circumstances. Although few signs of World War II remain, Guamanians find that their economic fortunes are inexorably tied to their former captors. Ninety percent of Guam's $800 million annual tourist income comes from Japan. While that may be a bright spot in an otherwise strained economy, it is the U.S. military expenditures in Guam that pose the iffy problems.

The $500 million a year the U.S. government pumps into Guam has grown after U.S. military forces were pulled out of the Philippines with an estimated 2,500 U.S. military personnel and dependents relocated in 1992 alone. Guam, though, really doesn't want more military, saying the military already occupy almost one-third of the island. But without the U.S. dollar from the military's presence, the Guamanian economy could collapse.

Guam in the 1990s has become fully absorbed into the Western way of life—automobiles, fast foods, welfare and beer. That, plus subservient employment in luxury hotels owned mostly by Japanese, has led to a breakdown in the traditional Chamorro family. Street crime is common and corruption in government has been rife in recent years. Guamanians blame it on their style of government—an unincorporated territory of the United States. But merely changing political status will not undo the root causes, cultural breakdown and loss of family traditions.

The rapid buildup of hotels, golf courses and other tourist attractions has dealt harshly with the environment. Almost uncontrolled in their development, they have caused excessive silting of streams and shoreline and inherent pollution of underground water supplies. More to the point, though, dozens of high-rise buildings along Tumon Bay have created a concrete jungle destroying the ambience of a tropical setting that was the earlier attraction for the tourist.

Years of dependence on the U.S. dollar have made Guamanians uncertain about, if not indifferent to, seeking a better way of life. History has not been kind to the Chamorros, but they have a better opportunity now to shape their own future than at any time since Magellan landed in 1521.

CHAPTER 13

PELELIU
Was It Bad Strategy?

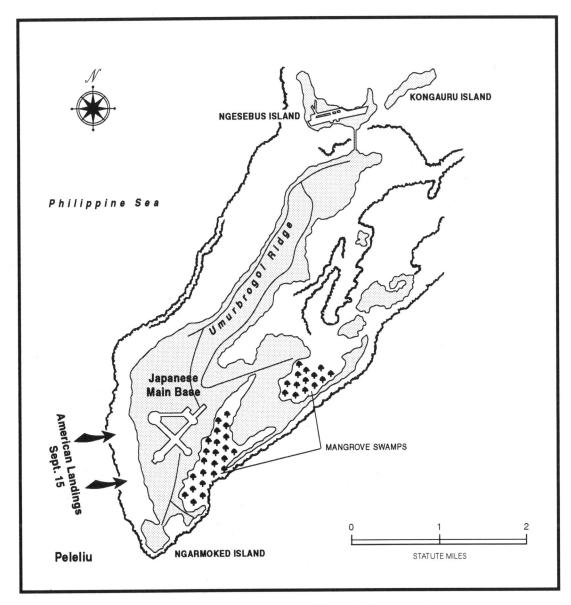

U.S. Operation STALEMATE - Peleliu Invasion

There was little in the Palau Islands of real strategic value to either the Japanese or United States other than their position 900 miles east of the Philippines. Yet they were to become a controversial steppingstone in General MacArthur's planned "return." In fact, some strategic planners even wondered whether the Philippines were essential to reaching America's ultimate target, Japan.

The U.S. Navy had already made solid advances westward through the Marshall and Caroline Islands and into the Marianas. From Saipan it was only another 1,400 miles via the Bonin Islands to Tokyo. Could not the Philippines be isolated and left to wither on the vine?

MacArthur would have none of it. He had left the Philippines with the pledge "I shall return," and he was still determined to land in the Philippines and free millions of loyal Filipinos from their Japanese captors. His passion rubbed off on others and it became a matter of honor for the United States to respect his pledge. Strategic plans were altered to fit.

Marine assault troops advancing on Peleliu under heavy fire from Japanese hidden in underbrush and caves.

A compromise strategy deleted the islands of Mindanao and Luzon from invasion plans as well as any thoughts of Formosa (Taiwan) or the China mainland. They did, however, include the capture of Palau to deny Japanese use of it during a landing on Leyte and give the Army Air Force another base within striking range of the Philippine Islands.

The Palaus are not a big group of islands, only 110 miles long in a north-south direction and about 12 miles wide from reef to reef. The main island of Babeldaob held airfields and a small protective garrison of some 5,000 Japanese. Koror Island was also headquarters for the Japanese South Seas Bureau, which administered all of the islands of former German Micronesia under the League of Nations mandate.

Little Peleliu, 25 miles south of Babeldaob, also had an airfield but with a larger defense garrison. Its smaller size (three by eight miles) implied an easier invasion. With plane and ship bombardment neutralizing the bigger island, U.S. forces could take Peleliu with ease, or so it was thought.

Six miles south of Peleliu lay Angaur Island, the only island in Palau with any natural resources. It was rich in phosphate. But Peleliu was to be the prime target and destined to become yet another assault into hell. Many still believe it was an unnecessary invasion and it certainly became more costly than planned.

Operation Stalemate Begins

The invasion force assigned to Operation Stalemate, an altogether unfortunate choice of code names, was the famed 1st Marine Division under Gen. William Rupertus—17,000 battle-hardened veterans from Guadalcanal and Cape Gloucester. Backing the Marines as a floating reserve was the Army's 81st "Wildcat" Division under Gen. Paul Mueller, an untried reserve outfit from Georgia and the Carolinas.

D-day was set for Sept. 15, 1944. Three days of ship bombardment, aircraft bombings and strafing and work by the Navy's underwater demolition teams prepared Peleliu for invasion. The confident commanding general said it would be over in three or four days. It actually lasted 72 days.

D-day landings were ragged in spite of past experience. The Marines, with their mortars and tanks, were landed through a rough surf. A shortage of tank-carrying landing craft and the loss of many amphtracs on the reef hampered the landing forces. Later, tainted drinking water from used diesel fuel barrels left the troops thirsty on a hot island.

Although beach defenses harassed the invaders, Peleliu's airfield was captured in 24 hours, and two days later Piper Cub spotting airplanes were using it as a base. Optimism prevailed to the extent that the force commander ordered the 81st Division reserve diverted to the assault and capture of Angaur.

Angaur was not only smaller than Peleliu, but was considerably flatter except for a prominent rise at its northwest corner called the Ramuldo. Here, wooded coral ridges rose 100 to 200 feet high and were honeycombed with natural caves that the Japanese had expanded in preparation for an attack. Like their Peleliu counterparts, the Japanese defenders of Angaur were hardened, experienced fighters.

Right: Fatigue, fear and futility are all mirrored in this Marine's face during the bloody fighting on Peleliu.

Bottom: Chaplain Rufus W. Oakley holds services for Marines within a few hundred yards of Japanese positions and well within mortar range.

Marine Pfc Douglas Lightheart, right, cradles a .30-cal. machine gun in his lap, while he and his buddy Pfc Gerald Churchby take time out from a mopping-up operation on Peleliu.

The assault on Angaur by the infantry began on September 17. Landings were made on the north and east sides of the two-mile-long by one-mile-wide island following the now accepted doctrine of sea and air bombardment. The initial landings met little resistance, and the Wildcats moved easily across the eastern plains of the phosphate island. But as they turned to the vine-covered ridges of the Ramuldo, the defense stiffened and it took four days of intensive, bloody fighting before organized resistance was broken. The Angaur battle cost the Japanese almost the entire 2,000-man garrison, while the Americans lost 200 men. The often-belittled Army reserves had given a good account of themselves. The bulk of the division returned to Peleliu to its original floating reserve role, but it took another 26 days to mop up the last diehard defenders.

Peleliu Turns Bloody

Meanwhile a cloud of uncertainty rose over the Marines' Peleliu assault. At first it appeared to go well against a known

heavily defended island. Estimates placed approximately 10,000 Japanese troops on Peleliu at the start of the invasion.

But hours after the attack started, it was evident that the Japanese under Colonel Nakagawa were not going to meet the invader on the beaches as in the past and extract casualties foot by foot as they retreated to the hills. Their tactics had changed. They had learned the futility of trying to stop determined landings at the beaches and now they opted to take advantage of the topography and geology of Peleliu.

Although the beaches were covered with pillboxes and other conventional obstacles to landings, the main Japanese defense line was an incredible maze of tunnels connecting the natural limestone caves in the Umurbrogol Ridge of the island.

The jagged coral ridges covered an area of only 500 by 1,000 yards but contained a labyrinth of tunnels and caverns too deeply buried for even 16-inch shells or 2,000-pound bombs to penetrate. The livability of the natural caves had been enhanced by professional miners. Some were cavernous enough to house 1,000 defenders. Each jagged ridge con-

The Japanese are able to pin down attacking Marines from their incredible maze of tunnels in the natural limestone caves of Peleliu Island.

Amphibious vehicles burn on the reef as Marines take shelter behind a "Duck" on a Peleliu beach.

tained its own complement of caves and tunnels enabling crossfire against the attackers as well as counterattacks at opportune moments.

Cave entrances were strategically located overlooking the airfield and the southern plateau forming the initial landing site. Other entrances looked out randomly around the compass enabling the defenders to sustain crossfire against any attackers who imprudently chose to attack any one of them. The defenders enjoyed all of the tactical advantages of controlling the high ground.

There was no way Peleliu could be secured without routing out by hand every last defender from the Umurbrogal caves. Direct assault with heavy firepower was getting the Marines nowhere. Tactics needed to be changed and they were. Newly acquired long-range flamethrowers mounted on amphtracs were tried. The principle was right, but not the vehicle. The flamethrowers were then shifted to Sherman tanks, which offered more protection to the crew and were better able to navigate the razor-sharp coral terrain. This worked.

The powerful flamethrower tanks finally enabled the Marines to secure the island in mid-October after one month, not four days, of intense fighting. They were then relieved by the 81st Division, who soon found out that the clean-up phase was just as dirty fighting as the assault phase. It took another six weeks to obliterate the tenacious and suicidal Japanese defenders. The security of the intricate tunnel-and-cave system is best illustrated by the fact that five Japanese stayed hidden and alive in the maze until September 1945, when they were induced to come out.

While the Japanese soldier had already proven himself a fanatical fighter, on Peleliu he was afforded a cheering section as far away as Tokyo. Unknown to the attackers at the time, Peleliu was in constant contact with military headquarters in Koror via a submarine cable. Not only was military advice sent to the defenders, but messages of support were given them, one coming from the emperor himself. It is no wonder that the Japanese garrison, faced with annihilation, was able to put up such a determined defense.

At best it was filthy, dirty fighting for both the Marines and infantry. Marine casualties numbered 1,252 dead and 5,274 wounded, while Army casualties, including the Angaur operation, numbered 542 dead and 2,736 wounded. The Marine casualties were twice those suffered at Tarawa. Imprecise estimates of Japanese dead defenders are a conservative 10,900 with another 302 captured. As in most other battles with the Japanese, there were no wounded left to count; it was a battle to the death only.

Peleliu Revisited

In the sunlight of the 1990s, Peleliu is still a shambles although the jungle growth has softened the edges of man's inhumanity to man. There are still relics of war to be found on this lightly populated island, including rusting tanks, amphtracs, live ammunition and booby traps.

The island is a historic shrine surmounted by a memorial erected to the memory of the Marines who lost their lives. The remains of many of the brave fighting men who lost their lives on the hot coral of this island are buried in the memorial cemetery. Within the maze of limestone caverns still lie the remains of many Japanese defenders, the task of recovering them too dangerous to accomplish without adding to the carnage of the original battle. There also are memorials to the Japanese who died.

The main village on Peleliu is Klouklubed, to the north of the notorious Umurbrogol Ridge. It is the birthplace of Palau's first democratically elected president, Haruo Remelik, who was assassinated in 1985. His grave is in the center of town. The island's population is now about 550. Peleliu's ancient name was Odesangel, meaning "beginning of everything," but for more than 12,000 men, it was the end.

Writer William Manchester summed it up appropriately: "Today it is the least accessible of the central Pacific's great battlefields, hidden away in the trackless deep like a guilty secret. It was a bad battle, fought at a bad place and a bad time, with an enemy garrison that could have been left to wither on the vine without altering the course of the Pacific war in any way."

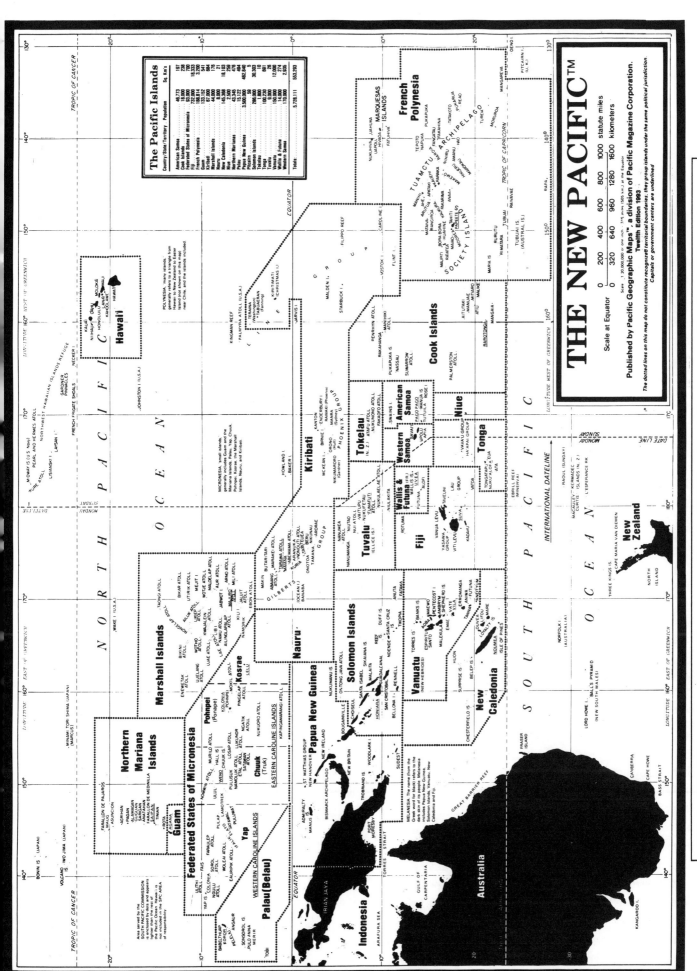

Wall-size (18" x 24") two-color copies of this map are available for US$5.00 each, including postage and handling in U.S. postal zones. For foreign orders, add US$2.00. Send check, cash or money order to Pacific Magazine, P.O. Box 25488, Honolulu, HI 96825.

by Bud Bendix

The raising of the flag on Mt. Surabachi, Iwo Jima. This famous photo was taken by Associated Press combat photographer Joe Rosenthal on Feb. 23, 1945.

When major fighting on Peleliu finally finished in October 1944, the war in the Pacific had barely 10 months to go until it ended. Yet there was much fighting to come, including some of the most historic events of the war. The Battle of Surigao Strait, at the time of the Leyte landings in the Philippines, became the last classic naval battle among capital ships using the battle line and the time-honored tactic called "crossing the T." Later, the Battle for Okinawa, on Japan's southern doorstep, saw the introduction and widespread use of kamikaze tactics—the suicide planes that caused much damage, especially to American warships. And

there was Iwo Jima and the many casualties on both sides before the raising of the Stars and Stripes on Mt. Surabachi, an event that produced a news photo that, today, is often used as a pictorial symbol of the entire Pacific war.

Many observers believed that the Philippines could (and should) have been bypassed, as it didn't provide a great strategic advantage any longer once the Americans had taken the Marianas, Guam and, later, Iwo Jima. Those islands provided bases that were close enough to the Japanese home islands to provide daily bombing raids. Formosa (Taiwan) was another consideration as was establishing a base on the

China coast. But General MacArthur wouldn't hear of it. He had promised the Filipinos he would return and return he did, amid the fanfare provided by a much-published news photo of him wading through the surf from a landing craft on Leyte. The Philippines campaign used up men, materiel and time that could have been put to use elsewhere. Nevertheless, it was a great emotional victory for which the Filipinos were grateful.

Okinawa, however, was a different story. It was to be the springboard for the invasion of the Japanese home islands themselves. Japan knew this and threw everything it could into Okinawa's defense, including the deadly kamikaze. But the Imperial Japanese Navy by this time simply did not exist. And Japan had lost most of its experienced pilots and air strength. Tens of thousands of soldiers had been expended fighting the United States and its allies in the earlier Pacific island battles. Although the fighting in and around Okinawa was fierce, there was never any doubt who would triumph.

As the Philippines started to plan for its rebuilding and eventual independence; as B-29 heavy bombers roared off runways in the Marianas to continue the aerial assault on Japan; as allied forces recovered ground from the Japanese in southeast Asia; as China began to see hope after years of oppression at the hands of her occupiers; as places like Guadalcanal and Tarawa became almost forgotten names; and with the war ended in Europe, all Allied military eyes focused on Japan. The Soviets and the British would be adding their strength to the war in the Pacific. Almost assuredly, the Japanese Empire would fall under the sheer weight of the great forces massing for the final chapter in the conflict.

But that chapter was to be rewritten. Allied leaders knew that landings in Japan would result in a long and bitter struggle, with heavy losses of life on both sides to add to the toll already taken since 1941. Peace overtures were made but went nowhere. It then was decided to use a new secret weapon, the most destructive device ever created by man —the atomic bomb. From Tinian in the Marianas, two American B-29 bombers carried the bombs that were dropped on Hiroshima and Nagasaki on August 6 and 9, 1945, with devastating results. They accomplished their purpose. There would be no more heavy losses of troops engaged in deadly combat. Five days after the Nagasaki bombing, Japan surrendered.

Japan was occupied by U.S. troops, its military machine was completely dismantled and, under the leadership of General MacArthur, it began the arduous task of rebuilding. Today, Japan is one of the industrial powers of the world and its investment in properties has restored its wealth, making it an international economic force that has few peers.

It may seem ironic that, today, the biggest source of income for a number of Pacific Island communities is from Japan, either in the form of visitors (as in Saipan and Guam; even in Hawaii it's significant) or in economic assistance (fisheries, agriculture development, power plants and other business enterprises in Tarawa, Guadalcanal and other battlegrounds of World War II). Japan has risen from the ashes. Its military ambitions are gone, although younger Japanese seem not to have been taught about World War II and its defeated imperialistic leaders. Yet its influence is felt in other ways that many see just as powerful as any war machine that existed under the banner of the Greater East Asia Co-Prosperity Sphere.

Earl Hinz is a graduate aeronautical engineer. Since his retirement in 1975, he has devoted his life to boats and the Pacific Ocean. He has sailed 40,000 miles, most of them in his 41-foot ketch, *Horizon*, his cruises taking him to the far reaches of the Pacific. He also has sailed in the biennial trans-Pacific yacht races to Honolulu and Tahiti.

A veteran of World War II, Hinz joined the U.S. Marine Corps Reserve in 1937 and was at Ewa Marine Air Base, Oahu, when the Japanese attacked Pearl Harbor on Dec. 7, 1941. Later, he was commissioned in the U.S. Naval Reserve as an aeronautical engineering officer. He left the Navy after the war with the rank of lieutenant commander.

Hinz began his career as a writer after his retirement, writing primarily on boating subjects. He has served as technical editor of *Sea Magazine* and has written regular columns on Pacific cruising for *Sea* and *Cruising World* magazines. He is a regular contributor to *Pacific Magazine* and has had articles in *Glimpses of Micronesia*, *Ocean Navigator*, *Western Boatman* and *Pacifica*. Hinz also has found the time to write six books—*Sail Before Sunset*, *Pacific Wanderer*, *Landfalls of Paradise*, *The Complete Book of Anchoring and Mooring*, *Understanding Sea Anchors* and *Drogues and The Offshore Log*.

A resident of Honolulu, he now lives aboard his trawler/yacht *Kumulani* (Hawaiian for "horizon") in the Ala Wai Boat Harbor.

Bud Bendix is a journalism graduate from Washington State University and has pursued a journalism career on newspapers in Washington state and Hawaii and in the corporate arena in Honolulu after serving on active duty in the U.S. Army from 1953 to 1955, which included one year in the Philippines. After retiring from GTE Hawaiian Tel, he joined *Pacific Magazine* as managing editor in January 1990. He has contributed articles to trade publications and was a correspondent for various U.S. Mainland newspapers for a number of years. He also has lectured to professional and college groups on writing and editing for publications. He is the author of *Hawaiian Telephone Company: The First 100 Years*.

Although he was too young to serve in the armed forces in World War II, Bendix has been a lifelong student of military history, particularly that of World War II in the Pacific. Like the author, he, too, has visited some of the Pacific battlegrounds in postwar years. Bendix has lived in Honolulu since 1958.